WHAT HAVE YOU DONE FOR ME LATELY?

A Politician Explains

REVISED EDITION

JEREMY AKERMAN

© 2022 Jeremy Akerman

All rights reserved. No part of this book may be reproduced or transmitted in any form or by any means, electronic or mechanical, including photocopying, or by any information storage or retrieval system, without permission in writing from the publisher.

Cover image and illustrations: Jeremy Akerman
Cover design: Rebekah Wetmore
Editor: Andrew Wetmore

ISBN: 978-1-990187-29-2
First edition (Lancelot Press) 1977
Revised edition April, 2022

MOOSE HOUSE
PUBLICATIONS

2475 Perotte Road
Annapolis County, NS
B0S 1A0

moosehousepress.com
info@moosehousepress.com

We live and work in Mi'kma'ki, the ancestral and unceded territory of the Mi'kmaw People. This territory is covered by the "Treaties of Peace and Friendship" which Mi'kmaw and Wolastoqiyik (Maliseet) People first signed with the British Crown in 1725. The treaties did not deal with surrender of lands and resources but in fact recognized Mi'kmaq and Wolastoqiyik (Maliseet) title and established the rules for what was to be an ongoing relationship between nations. We are all Treaty people.

Also by Jeremy Akerman

Black Around the Eyes
First published by McLelland & Stewart, 1981
Second edition by Moose House Publications, 2022

Outsider
Moose House Publications, 2022

Dedication

This book is dedicated to the memory of Aneurin Bevin and Paul Matheson;

to the many others—in and out of politics—who have inspired me to plough, seed and harvest in stony ground;

and to George Clease, without the benefit of whose clarity of analysis and expression I might never have become interested in politics, let alone an active participant.

"Will you vote for me in the election?"
"I'm not sure I will."
"What? You may not vote for me? But I paved your road. I found you a job. I helped you find a house. I fixed your mother's pension. I helped your son when he was in trouble. I filled out your income tax form and I won your compensation case!"
"Yes, but what have you done for me lately?"

- old political joke

Foreword to the 2022 edition

Please treat this book as if it were a document revealed in a recently-opened time capsule. It reflects its time, and I have changed nothing in it except for correcting one small error in fact. However, in the 46 years since I wrote *What Have You Done for Me Lately*, much has changed.

Certainly my views on many subjects have undergone the tempering of hard experience. I was still young, idealistic and naive. Today, I would not write as I did then about some of the people, and some of the practices. The biggest change is that almost everybody I mentioned in the book is now dead, something which fills me with sadness because their ranks included great characters and remarkable personalities.

Then, the remuneration of Members of the Legislature was modest. Indeed when I was first elected, six years before the book came out, all we received was $7,500 a year including all expenses. At last report (in round figures), the basic indemnity was $89,000 with an extra $2-3,000 if they are chairpersons of committees. The premier gets another $112,000, the Speaker and Leader of the Opposition another $50,000, The caucus chairs of each party get another $10,000 and the party whips an additional $5,000. House Leaders receive an extra $10,000 and Deputy House Leaders $5,000.

It is difficult to explain the rationale for some of

these figures: For example, what does a Deputy House Leader do and, whatever that might be, is it worth an additional $5,000? Does chairing a meeting of the caucus a few times a week really require an extra $10,000 to enable him/her to bear the heavy burden?

In addition, MLAs have publicly financed constituency offices and staff. Everything combined, the average non-Halifax-based MLA who has no additional title is costing the taxpayers something in the order of $110,000, depending upon where he/she lives.

And why have all these subsidiary payments come into being? There are two explanations, the first being that it provides a patronage system for the party leader, who is able to purchase the special loyalty of six or seven members of his caucus. The second is that, at first glance, the taxpayer will see and remember only the base figure, and be unaware that many MLAs are actually making much more.

The major difference between 1970 ($7,500) and 2022 ($110,000) is that then all but two MLAs (who were not members of cabinet) were part time; today, I think, all MLAs are full time. It has to be asked if the province is the better for that change.

I used to argue this point with Gerald Regan, who maintained that persons who had a stake in the community other than their political future brought something special to the House, and that when all MLAs became professional politicians the House would lose that special quality. I claimed that public affairs were becoming so complex and so many new problems were confronting constituents that only a full time MLA could handle the work.

But to a significant extent it could be argued that today's MLA has *less* to do, because over the years the government has surrendered many of its powers and responsibilities to arms-length boards, agencies and commissions. The Nova Scotia Utility and Review Board is just one, if the most egregious, example of this, where immense powers have been transferred to non-elected officials from whose decisions an ordinary Nova Scotia only has redress if he/she can afford to appeal to a court.

So, on balance I think that Jerry Regan was somewhat more correct than I was, but it is too late to turn back the clock. For better or worse, the "gentleman" politicians who were also practising lawyers, doctors, pharmacists, teachers, farmers—and who brought their daily experiences to bear on their work as MLAs—have largely gone the way of the dodo, and the "professional" politician is here to stay.

Also different in some ways is the House of Assembly. New portraits have been added to the walls —Dexter, Adams and Atwell have joined Porter, Fielding, Johnstone and Tupper. Many of the rules and procedures I described in the book have undergone significant changes, most of them as a result of the work in 1979-80 of a committee comprised of Arthur Donahoe, Hugh Tinkham and myself.

There are far fewer good speakers than used to be the case, and no great orators (although Gary Burrill comes closest). Most speeches are read from scripts, and even questions to ministers are read off a piece of paper, neither of which Paul MacEwan or I would ever have dreamt of doing. A few notes on the back of an envelope was all we needed because we believed that, as representatives of our constituents, our primary duty was to know enough about their problems to be able to speak about them extemporaneously.

Reading speeches is still, I think, officially prohibited in the House of Assembly, but that rule is more honoured in the breach than in the observance, the euphemism "extensive notes" being employed. This has arisen, at least in part, because increased party discipline has required MLAs to strictly adhere to the party line *as written by staff*, something we would never have tolerated.

Not long ago, a highly vocal, a feisty, seemingly independent-minded MLA complained to me that she wanted to make a particular point in the House, but her leader wouldn't let her. I was astounded, told her she was an MLA and could say whatever she liked, especially if her constituents would support her if there were any fall-out. She looked at me blankly, saying she thought that only speech approved by her leader was permissible under the rules.

In the days I describe in this book, I loved the House and wanted its sessions to last forever, because I was never at a loss to get on my hind feet and give speeches on every subject under the sun. But the length of sessions has been severely reduced, largely because of a dramatic change in government's attitude to the Assembly. Then, the government relished the opportunity to put its case and vigorously defend its positions; now it seems they want to say as little as possible and get out as fast as they can. Even some opposition MLAs have told me they want the Legislature sessions to be over quickly so they can go home. One even took foreign vacations while the House was in session.

Some things, however, have not changed in the intervening 46 years.

Unchanged is the power of the media to enhance

or damage a politician. If anything it is greater now than it was then, while at the same time the quality of reporting is probably at an all-time low. Sensationalism still rules the day and the laziness or the illiteracy of the media precludes them from doing any in-depth analysis. If a minister were to hold a press conference in the Uniacke Room explaining his bill to completely reorganize municipal government and education in Nova Scotia, while at the same time an opposition MLA were holding a press conference in the Red Room to accuse the premier of having a girlfriend on the side, the Red Room would be crammed to capacity, while in the Uniacke Room the minister would be talking to...nobody.

Politicians are still politicians and have as their primary function getting re-elected. Some, if not many, will do and say whatever it takes to accomplish that goal, including completely reversing themselves. Few, if any in recent years have said what they really think, and even fewer have defied their party. That is because, in a world where no-one is allowed to be offended, they know that the smallest deviation from political correctness will get them expelled from their party, and that for ridiculously slight indiscretions they will be obliged to provide grovelling apologies to all and sundry.

Apart from Elizabeth Smith-McCrossin, I am struggling to recall when last a Member of the Legislature stood on principle for anything.

My view that there are ways in which we could encourage a diversity of opinion in the legislature has not changed. I still do not believe that every vote should be subjected to party discipline. If votes were categorized by their importance, the interests of constituents and the personal beliefs of members could be accommodated without any danger to the continuation of responsible government.

As each measure came up for a vote, the government and opposition whips would underscore the title of each with one, two or three lines. A one-line whip would mean the vote is "free", a two-line whip would mean the party would like you to vote with the boss, but understands if you have personal or constituency objections; a three-line whip would mean vote with the party or else.

This system would preserve the government on confidence votes and important legislation, while allowing back-benchers to let off steam and get some publicity in their ridings.

If the foregoing suggests that I am unduly critical of MLAs, I must add that I think the overwhelming majority of them are suitably motivated and serve the province well often under difficult circumstances. I have an abiding understanding of and liking for politicians of all parties, and am still in contact with almost a hundred of them through XMLAS, the Association of Former Members of the Nova Scotia Legislature, of which I am founder and president.

And when all is said and done, love 'em or hate 'em, politicians will always be with us and we will always have a need for their work if we wish to preserve our democracy. But we should never hesitate to ask, "What have you done for me lately?"

JBA, 2022

Introduction to the 1977 edition

Since I was elected to the Nova Scotia Legislature in 1970 a number of people, including other politicians, have expressed the desire for some kind of brief handbook to explain politics and politicians to the people. Politicians of my acquaintance have expressed particular frustration over the many misunderstandings harboured by the public about political life, especially by school students. A friend suggested to me that I attempt to write such a book which might be useful and informative for schools and general public alike. This is the attempt.

This book is very short. It is deliberately so as I have made a very conscious effort to reduce to as few words as possible an account which would give an idea of the character and flavour of political life without being tedious. I hope I have succeeded.

Jeremy Akerman
Glace Bay, Nova Scotia
June 1976

Contents

    Foreword to the 2022 edition 7
    Introduction to the 1977 edition 13
1: Open Season 17
2: The Candidate 23
3: The Member 37
4: The House 49
5: The Constituency 63
6: The Leader 79
7: Private Conscience, Public Will and the Party Line 87
8: The Power of the Press 99
9: Policy, Patronage and Cash 107
10: Pros and Cons 115
    About the author 123

Jeremy Akerman

1: Open Season

The season on politicians runs from January to December every year. No license is required. Virtually any weapons are permissible, and no special clothing, equipment, training or knowledge is necessary. Restrictions on how, when and where politicians may be hunted are few. It is an ideal sport and therefore small wonder that so many enjoy it.

The hunted creature is a strange breed. It is widely known for its extravagant promises, none of which are ever kept, its barefaced lies, its practise of lining its own pockets, its ability to push buttons, pull strings and "fix" things, all the while living a life of riotous indulgence. This creature may be blamed for everything which goes wrong from problems in the far east entirely beyond its control to the dogs knocking over the garbage cans next door. I have even heard the government blamed for the weather ("What the hell can you expect from the Liberals?" asked the friend to whom I complained about a fierce blizzard). Once, a caller left me in no doubt that he was holding me responsible for a train which had become derailed some fifty miles away, while, on another occasion I was roundly condemned for not "making" the local newspaper print Gaelic poetry.

"You're all crooks and you're all in it together," I have been told and, while most would not put it as bluntly as that, I have a strong feeling that thousands share this opinion.

I am not a hunter, but I am told that very occasionally, under special circumstances, the hunted creature will sometimes turn on the hunter and give him a little dose of his own medicine. This little book represents a mild reprimand to the hunter; to gently take his gun away for a few minutes and to quietly reason with him, to explain some things about politics and politicians of which he may be unaware. I will try to tell him that while there are unquestionably some liars and crooks in politics, the majority are not; that while there are some who have become rich through politics, most have not; that while many politicians are stupid and incompetent, it is dangerous, if not unfair, to generalize about an entire profession.

I will ask him not to pass judgment when he has not seen all the evidence and has not heard all the witnesses. Most importantly, I will ask him to consider if the politicians are not a reflection of those who put them in office and of the times in which they live and to which they are trying to respond.

Politicians are charged with certain responsibilities and are delegated to make serious—often far-ranging—decisions. If it can be shown that their decisions are bad or that they have failed to discharge their responsibilities they should be condemned.

What Have You Done for Me Lately?

Politicians who demonstrate stupidity or incompetence should, of course, be criticized. However, I feel it is important for the health of public affairs that criticism be warranted and that it not be misdirected. The extent to which criticism of politicians is misdirected or undeserved is probably the extent to which the public generally possesses a lack of understanding of politicians and the political process. A great many people simply do not know how parliament works, which levels of government are supposed to provide which services, and what kind of work their elected member should be doing.

Many see the life of the politician as one of luxury and glamour, some as a living hell. There are extremely few and fleeting moments when it may be both of these, but, generally speaking, the politician's life is neither all black nor all white. There are many rewards, scores of disadvantages; there are moments of exaltation and of utter despair; there are times of profound gloom and of hysterical mirth. The politician is first, last and always a human being and his profession is one in which human strength and human frailty is the every day bread and butter.

Misconceptions about politicians and their work are numerous and an entire book could alone be devoted to their enumeration. A few examples must suffice:

A Member of the Provincial Legislature is stopped on the street in mid summer and asked angrily why he is not "in Ottawa." It is not the easiest task in the world to draw him away from the bustling passers-

Jeremy Akerman

by to delineate the difference between the federal and provincial representatives, nor yet to explain that in mid-summer it is unlikely that either Parliament or the Legislature would be in session.

A Federal Member of Parliament arrives home on the weekend to be roundly condemned for a motion passed in his absence by the local municipal council. The M. P. tells the constituent that he has no "control over" the town council and that the person should complain to his municipal councillor. The constituent mutters loudly about "passing the buck."

The day after a member has been elected he is approached by persons who fully suppose that he now has instant access to public funds, not only for his own use, but for theirs, too.

While the Legislature is in session, perhaps debating a matter of hot controversy, the member's wife will receive a call at home demanding to know why the member is not in the constituency. "He's got no business in Halifax," complains the constituent. "We elected him to be here when we need him!"

On another day when the House is sitting, the member may have an important meeting with a delegation, or may have to attend a committee which may be sitting at the same time as the House. A constituent who is in town happens to drop into the gallery and is incensed that his representative is not present. "We pay him $15,000 a year to sit in that place and where was he?" the constituent asks his work buddies. "Probably living it up on the town!"

A constituent learns from the newspaper that a

What Have You Done for Me Lately?

certain bill received "first reading" the day before. He asks his member to explain the contents and purpose of the bill and, when the member is unable to do so, demands, "Why weren't you listening?" The member begins to tell him that when a bill is "read" it is not really read at all and that he, as a backbencher, will not know what the bill is all about until a printed copy is inserted in his billbook the next day. The constituent is unconvinced. "What kind of doubletalk is that? Either the bill is read or it's not read!"

Again, a constituent may be in the public gallery and takes exception to some remarks made by the speaker. He asks his representative, "Why didn't you get up right then and there and answer that SOB?" The member's attempts to explain that the rules only allow a member to speak once on a motion and that he gave his speech two days earlier get short shift from the constituent, who tells him, "We don't do things that way back home in the local union."

A constituent who is unaware that often even a cabinet minister is unable to produce employment for his strongest supporters is highly indignant that his own member, a backbencher, will not come up with a job for his son right on the spot.

Finally, one of the most frustrating. The member is asked to reverse the decision of a court. Gentle reminders that the person pleaded guilty and that there is a separation between the legislature and the judiciary are seldom, under the circumstances, received with kindness.

Jeremy Akerman

On the other side of the ledger: a pensioner, with tears in her eyes, offers a crumpled dollar bill as thanks for the member having solved her problems; a group of men at a trades training course proudly present the member with a piece of furniture in which they have all had a hand because "you fought to stop them cutting off our course"; a woman calls on Christmas Eve: "Do you remember me? I went to you about my crippled boy three years ago. Because of what you did he's getting along fine now and can you believe it—he'll be going to university this year. God bless you!"

This book is an attempt to describe some of the aspects of a politician's life as I have observed them over a decade of active participation. Most of my illustrations are drawn, naturally enough, from my experience at the provincial level in Nova Scotia, but also to some extent from my knowledge of federal members of parliament and from my involvement at the national level in my own party. I hope to show that, basically, politics can be a decent and honourable calling, and, while there are good and bad practitioners, it is extremely dangerous for the public to see politicians as villains or messiahs.

So, lay aside your guns for a short while and take a look at the all too human beings who are doing a job which has to be done—a job which the public asked them to do.

2: The Candidate

The greatest influence exerted by the ordinary rank and file members of a political party is probably to be found in the nomination of the candidate. The party hierarchy may try to persuade them to nominate Mr. Smith, but if they prefer Ms. Jones then she will probably be the candidate. Unless the nominating meeting is rigged or the party bosses really turn on excessive pressure, party headquarters will have little to say about who the party candidate will be in a particular riding. Sometimes pressure from above will ensure the rejection of the establishment choice as a result of backlash which is generated.

Recently, I was chatting with an MLA of another party in one of the western provinces about a forthcoming by-election in a seat which his party had held for years. Since his party leader did not then have a seat in the legislature I indicated that I assumed the leader would be the candidate. "Not likely," replied the indignant MLA. "They don't want *him* down there—they want one of their own!"

For years party leaders have attempted to secure so-called "quality" candidates and impose them on local constituencies. Sometimes they have succeeded; more often they have failed because the

Jeremy Akerman

local party members are the best judges of the kind of person the area needs to represent it and, moreover, the kind of person they feel they can elect.

Sometimes there are memorable fights at the nominating meeting in which the "local" candidate and the "establishment" choice jockey all night for the party's nomination. One of the most colourful in recent times must be the nomination of the affable Harry How, Conservative (some say independent) MLA for Kings South, who is said to have run the "establishment" choice an incredible number of ballots, finally capturing the nomination in the not-so-early hours of the morning.

Supporters of opposing parties always greet such occasions with great glee, opining that a "split" will develop as a result of the nomination contest and will reduce the nominee's chances of election. This is seldom the case, and, in my experience, wherever such a split was reported to have developed as a result of a so-called schism between the "locals" and the hierarchy, the party suffering the "split" went on to win the polls.

When the candidate has received the nomination of his party, whether by acclamation, as is usually the case, or in a heated contest, his troubles have only just begun. He or she now has to go out and convince the electorate at large that he should be elected—and preferably with a large majority. In order to do that the candidate has to drink approximately a thousand cups of tea, knock on at least as many doors, keep his or her spouse from going in-

What Have You Done for Me Lately?

sane over the number of calls to the house, mediate differences of opinion and petty jealousies between various party workers, listen politely while being insulted to his face and, above all else, keep smiling!

After a few weeks of the campaign many candidates wonder why they ever entertained such an idiotic idea as running for public office and swear that if they are unsuccessful they will never do it again. Invariably those who say they will never run again are those who time after time offer themselves for slaughter.

These repeating candidates are those for whom great praise should be reserved, for they are generally the utterly devoted party supporters who will not see the party let down and are usually persons who are running in constituencies where their party has slim chances of success.

Other candidates have a variety of motives in standing for office. These motives range from having thought "it was a good idea at the time", to being told they will be cabinet material should their party form the government, to those who are looking for a government job and see their candidacy as a way of ingratiating themselves with the powers-that-be, to those who genuinely believe it is their civic duty to make themselves available to serve the people.

An election campaign is a time of tremendous stress for a candidate. Some are almost disabled by the pressures, others thrive on the excitement and artificial pace of events. Others, like myself, have a love-hate relationship with the campaign: they dread its arrival, enjoy it while it is in progress, thank heaven when it is over, then feel sad because it will be so long before the next one.

The campaign is an excellent opportunity to do many things and to meet many people, an opportunity which, under normal circumstances, does not present itself to a person unless he is elected. It is a time for making many new friends and for finding out just how reliable the old friends are. It is a time when just about everything that can go wrong does go wrong and when, having planned down the minutest detail, one discovers that, for a million strange reasons, all the plans have to be changed—often at the eleventh hour!

The most intriguing and often frustrating aspects of a campaign are connected with gossip, blackmail and soothsaying. Gossip is a staple diet in the committee rooms, where various party supporters indicate that they heard that so-and-so heard that candidate A is "slipping" or that candidate B has "peaked too soon" or that there has been a "backlash" against the candidate for a certain public statement he has made.

The blackmail enters the picture when some voters (fortunately very few) inform the candidate that unless he or she does this or that they will desert the party and will take fifty votes with them. It is truly amazing that individuals who normally would not even be able to influence their spouses, at election time suddenly acquire a huge a following which they are able to direct in any way they may or-

What Have You Done for Me Lately?

der. Thus the candidate is told to be nice to Mr. A because he "controls thirty votes" and not to offend Mrs. B because she has a "block of twenty votes."

In my experience this is largely nonsense. While some persons in a community are influential and could sway some voters in their direction, the vast majority of the electorate are going to make up their own minds.

The soothsaying manifests itself by the almost daily predictions of the outcome, with some party supporters keeping a daily score on a bulletin board. Often the soothsayers will write their predictions on dirty scraps of paper and seal them in an envelope not to be opened until election night. If there was not far too much other activity to preoccupy the workers after the polls had closed there would be a great many red faces around when the envelopes were opened.

Different candidates react differently to events and trends which may develop during the campaign. If confronted with the feeling that the campaign is "slipping", many will furiously throw themselves into the fight with redoubled vigour, while others will crumble and mentally throw in the towel. The campaign manager and other key workers, among their many other tasks, may constantly have to reassure the candidate that nothing is decided until all the ballots are counted, while at the same time trying to persuade the more enthusiastic supporters that it is not "in the bag."

Campaign managers—and, far too often, candidates, too—daily have to deal with a variety of complaints and disputes. New campaign techniques being introduced are often met with a surly resistance: "We never did it that way here and it won't work now." Attempts to allocate resources where the committee feels they are most needed often incite open rebellion: "How come poll 36 has three cars and mine's only got one? Unless we get another car, there's going to be trouble!" And so on.

A candidate passing through his headquarters is likely to encounter one or all of the following snippets of conversation:

"I don't care if you do have ten workers for poll 39, I always worked in that poll!"

"If Johnny (the candidate) doesn't get down to Ward three right now fifty votes are going to fly away."

"Three times I asked Jim to put that blankety sign up and its still not up!"

"You gotta go up and see my grandmother on the hill. She says if you don't go she won't go out to vote."

"Fella here says he has information that could blow the lid off the campaign. Better listen to him, Johnny, there are thirteen votes in his family."

"We lost two votes on French Street. A dog bit Bill so he kicked it. The owners are real mad."

"Mrs. MacNeil called. She said to tell you you were lovely on TV last night."

"What do you mean, did I get the hall? I thought you were supposed to get the hall!"

"The flight is cancelled? Oh my God!"

What Have You Done for Me Lately?

"The newspaper says if we don't pay up now they'll cut us off any advertising for the rest of the campaign."

"Be reasonable, Mr. Smith. He can't be in three places at once."

"Your wife called, Johnny. She wants to know if you'll be home any time this week."

"I don't care what Provincial Office says. I'm running this show. You just tell Provincial Office to—"

"Tell Joe that if I don't get another $500 this thing is going right down the tube!"

"Surprise, everyone! You know Henry was looking after Ward Four? His wife says he's been missing for three days. Must have broke his keg."

"Now, I know you're not too busy or anything, Johnny, so here's old Mrs. MacDonald. She wants to tell you about her pension case. Goes right back to 1924."

The candidate escapes, clutching his ulcers.

Elections are usually held on the first or second day following a weekend so you have that brief, artificial lull on the Sunday when the committee rooms are closed and only a few die-hards linger in the back room, sitting, smoking, worrying like generals before a battle. They rack their brains for some detail they may have forgotten, they check and recheck their lists of workers, they hope the weather will stay fine, and they pray that John Jones will not have one of his "queer spells" until after the polls have closed.

Election day itself usually starts with a short but

Jeremy Akerman

frantic period of telephone calling to "key people" and a final, hasty re-allocation of personnel. Everyone but the candidate, the campaign manager and a few office staff leave, and calm descends.

The calm, which is unbearable, may last until after lunch, when, having dispatched the candidate to tour the polls or to drag out some reluctant voters, the remaining people nervously chew on limp hamburgers.

"I don't understand it," says the campaign manager, making his twelfth cup of coffee. "Why is it so quiet? Something's gone wrong. Why aren't they calling in? What the hell are they doing?"

He dispatches someone to "do the rounds", knowing in his heart that his courier will bring back tales of complete collapse of the organization, of unmanned polls everywhere, and of opposition tactics which have "snatched" victory from them at the last moment.

The messenger returns, nonchalantly reports everything running smoothly, and eats the remains of the campaign manager's hamburger. The latter smiles nervously and inwardly compliments himself on his brilliant organizational ability.

He rejoices that there are no problems, but, deep in his heart, he knows it will not last.

It doesn't. Towards three or four in the afternoon all hell breaks loose. The pressure increases due to large numbers returning from work, now wanting to vote and calling for transportation. The people who have told the workers at least three times they will

What Have You Done for Me Lately?

"vote later" still have not gone to the polls. A worker who was supposed to relieve Fred in poll 22 has failed to materialize.

The car serving poll 18 has broken down. John Jones has had one of his "queer spells." Bob's wife says he has gone fishing. Scores of voters now find they are not on the voters' list: in urban areas where they are not allowed to be "sworn in" they become enraged; in rural areas where they can be "sworn in" they protest that taking the necessary oath is an insult to them and they will not vote.

Workers in poll 21 are mad because they heard that the candidate visited other polls but did not go to theirs. The sandwiches destined for poll 5 are sent to poll 61 where they have already received two lunches.

Calls come in from people who want their final pep talk with the candidate or they will not vote. Disreputable characters who have either voted already or have no intention of voting at all say that they "were told" they could get five dollars if they came to headquarters, and on failing to identify their mysterious informant are sent on their way.

A call advises that some one "has got to" Cecil, who will, therefore, not be at his station in poll 40. Two calls come in to say that "something funny is going on" at poll 32.

By this time, the candidate, who is convinced that he will receive zero votes, and the campaign manager, who has chewed his fingernails to the bone, are both ready to sign themselves into a mental hospital.

But it is not over yet.

The tempo further increases and the last hour before the polls close becomes a nightmare. Telephones are ringing continuously, people are running in and out, paper is flying everywhere, men are shouting, women are arguing, predictions are being changed by the minute, and, at that very moment an out-of-town visitor who slept late that morning drops by just to say, "Hello."

From his reception he concludes that the people here are not very friendly!

The polls close. It is too late to correct the mistake. It is too late to clarify a controversial statement. It is too late to pay one more call to the Smiths, who would not go to vote.

The candidate is utterly alone.

Supporters clap him on the back and tell him he did a good job—someone tactlessly adds, "under the circumstances." His campaign manager—who has been snarling at him for weeks—tells him he was great to work with and that nobody could have done any more or better.

He knows it is not true. He knows that he was wrong to offend the Smiths, he was stupid to have made the statement about abortion, he was idiotic to have spent too much time in Ward One, he was insane to have stayed away from the Citizens Improvement Association meeting, he was totally, utterly out of his mind ever to have considered the nomination in the first place.

The results start coming in; in some constituen-

What Have You Done for Me Lately?

cies with a great flood with which it is impossible to keep abreast, in others with a painful slowness.

There are usually two kinds of election results: those which show a "trend" which is maintained until the end, and those which "see-saw" back and forth, being decided only by the last few polls. To those candidates whose election results are in the latter category goes my heartfelt sympathy, for the agony must be indescribable.

I think of my colleague, Paul MacEwan, who in 1970 won by only 61 votes in a "see-saw" battle, and former Liberal MLA Lloyd MacDonald, who scraped through with a bare 19 votes. But it was a picnic for them compared with the agonies of former Tory Welfare Minister Gordon Tidman, who had to sit through the night to discover that the result of the last poll tied him with his opponent.

In the event Tidman was declared elected by the casting vote of the returning officer (and thus, temporarily, was able to deprive the incoming new Liberal government of a majority in the House), but was subsequently ejected when the election was declared void.

Those whose election results establish early "trends" do not suffer the same agonies, but they still suffer. Those who are leading in such trends (notwithstanding the cries from supporters: "He can't catch you now, Johnny!") experience what feels like the loss of their intestines at the sudden thought that in the polls not yet heard from the vote will dramatically swing to the opponent and sweep him into office. Indeed, my friend Frank Boone must have experienced feelings worse than this when, in the Cape Breton West by-election in September 1976, he was defeated by the results of the last three polls after having held the lead all night.

Similarly, those who are trailing in the results pray that an act of Divine Providence will transform all uncounted votes into expressions of favour for themselves. Such a dramatic turn of events does occasionally happen, but it is extremely rare.

It is not quite over. To the victors go all the spoils; to the losers further sadness and hurt.

The victor stays where he is and awaits the arrival of his unsuccessful opponents to congratulate him. It is a glorious feeling to see them appear to shake your hand. It is complete wretchedness to have to go to them, force your way through the throng of their jubilant supporters, suffer the few unkind catcalls, and make for the smiling conqueror.

When I did precisely this following the 1968 Federal election, in which I was well and truly beaten by Tory Donnie MacInnis, I found that he had already left. I failed to find him at home and finally paid my tribute at the local television station.

Two years later, when I was victorious in a "trend" result, former cabinet minister Layton Fergusson—an incumbent for nearly fifteen years—had to push his way through my cheerful supporters to shake my hand. It was a tough thing to do and I admired him for it, because I knew exactly what it felt like.

Even that is not the end. There is still the workers'

What Have You Done for Me Lately?

party. At the victor's party the hall is packed with well-wishers (including some the candidate had not seen during the campaign and whom he strongly suspects worked for one of his opponents), the atmosphere is euphoric, everyone is all smiles. To the loser's party go only the hard-core faithful (and even some of them are so heart-broken they cannot bear to go), the atmosphere is downcast, the faces are exceedingly glum.

The winner tells the throng it is a great victory and thanks his workers; the loser tells his sparse gathering that this is only a temporary setback and that the next campaign begins as of that very moment.

It seldom, if ever, does.

For whatever reasons, party and personal, the voters have spoken. In the days ahead there will be recriminations and speculation as to what might have happened "if only...", but it cannot be changed until the next time, which may be as much as four years away.

It only remains for the candidates to go home to bed, the losers sick at heart, the winner wearily happy. The latter is also expectant, for he is now The Member and faces an interesting, frustrating, exhilarating and totally unique new way of life.

Jeremy Akerman

3: The Member

Some persons are very blasé about being elected to office for the first time. These gallants who, I suggest, are in a small minority, shrug casually that the result was exactly what they expected and that it is no big deal. Most awaken the day after the election with an indefinable feeling of well-being and propriety. They may stroll around town accepting the wishes of passers-by and luxuriate for a while in the warm sense of actually having been wanted by so many of their fellow citizens.

A few became intoxicated with their success and start dashing about giving advice and opinions (and sometimes orders) even where they have not been solicited. Others become nervous about the new responsibilities and worry about their ability to shoulder them. Some immediately become political animals in the truest sense and commence plans to double their majority in the next election.

These latter creatures may be assisted into a mild paranoia by friends who may tell them of all the "lucky breaks" which conspired to elect them, and by enemies who tell them that "it was a fluke" and will not occur again.

Jeremy Akerman

Usually, newly elected members of the party which forms the government will be most elated; not only have they received the approbation of their constituents, but their party is "in power".

If the party is newly elected to power, especially if the defeated government had been in for many years, there may be an additional tendency to gloat "we are the rulers now!"

Whether elected to the team of a new government or of one which has been returned to office, the new member may have ideas of getting into the cabinet, of paving all the roads in his district or of obtaining dozens of grants for local organizations. He may be able to realize some of these ambitions, but, often as not, he will be disappointed.

It may be that his area is already "top heavy" with cabinet ministers, in which case the Premier might gently inform him that while he is of the very highest calibre and eminently suited for the cabinet, "geography is against him"; or other religious and ethnic factors may be held up as having conspired against him.

These factors still play a part in the selection of cabinets (less so today than in years gone by), but invariably ability and, more importantly, seniority will decide.

For the newly elected member who finds himself in opposition, there may be visions of "hammering that crowd" or getting pet schemes adopted by sheer force of logic and oratory. He will find that he may be able "to hammer" the government, but if he thinks his oratory and logic will convince the administration to adopt his ideas very often he is about to be sadly disillusioned, and, in fact, he may find to his even greater chagrin that he is unable even to convince his own party caucus!

Soon the members, new and veteran, government and opposition, are summoned to the capital by the Lieutenant Governor to take the oath (The Lieutenant Governor, the queen's representative in the province, actually does very little summoning and the vast majority of the things which are done in his name are done by and on the orders of the government).

They troop into a large room (in Nova Scotia, the historic "Red Room" where formerly resided the now defunct equivalent of the provincial senate), they nod and shake hands all over the place, pledge their allegiance and kiss the Bible.

They are now ready to take their seats.

While the Canadian parliamentary system is modelled very closely on the British system, in the Canadian House of Commons and in provincial legislatures the members actually do have seats allotted to them. At Westminister, the "mother of parliaments", unless the member is a minister or a senior opposition member there are occasions when he may not be able to get a seat, as the task of cramming over 600 MPs into a chamber smaller than the one at Ottawa would be difficult even for experienced sardine canners. In Canada, not only does he get a seat but he gets a desk as well, and these desks are arranged in rows on either side of the central Aisle. The more junior the member is the further to the back of the chamber will he be placed, the party leaders deciding who sits where, with the Premier and the Leader of the Opposition facing each other in the front row on either side.

In the middle of the House is the Table, on which rests the mace (symbol of the Royal authority) and around which sit the clerks who keep all the records and, sometimes, help interpret the rules. On the other side of the table, opposite the main doors, sits the Speaker on an elevated throne. The Speaker is usually a member elected for the Government side and is supposed to be the impartial chairman and judge of the conduct of debates.

This, then, is the setting into which the members move to hear the Speech from the Throne, which is read by the Lieutenant Governor and is supposed to outline the major points of the government's forthcoming legislative program (at Ottawa, the Governor General delivers this speech in the Senate; at Westminister, the Queen gives it in the House of Lords).

When the Governor has departed, an Address in Reply to the Speech from the Throne is then moved and seconded by two government backbenchers who praise the administration and express their unshakable belief that all will be rosy in the days ahead. The Leaders of the opposition parties then say why the Speech from the Throne is a pitiful document, the Premier denies it, and the House settles down to business.

What Have You Done for Me Lately?

Who are these people? Who are these members who have been sent here by the voters to conduct the public's business for them? They come in many shapes and sizes.

My fellow member of the Nova Scotia Legislature, Liberal Frank Bezanson, has cleverly categorised the members into three groups: "The Jawbones", "The Knucklebones", and "The Backbones." The Jawbones, he says, are those who talk but do nothing else; the Knucklebones those who let others do the work; and the Backbones those who are really sincere and hardworking.

There is a lot to commend the Bezanson Parliamentary Rating System (BPRS), but I do not feel it is really adequate because it is not sufficiently comprehensive. There are many "types" of members and a member may possess the characteristics of more than one type. The reader shall be the judge of which types he or she prefers.

The first type is the rarest. This is the "Statesman", and let me hastily add I have no personal knowledge of this type, because it is so rare. The Statesman combines the qualities of wit, persuasiveness, kindness, oratorical ability, leadership, honesty, fairness and an ability to see and to concede the strong points in the arguments of another. He must also be constantly true to his principles and must place the welfare of his country before that of himself and his party. It is small wonder that such a paragon of virtue is to be found only once in a hundred years!

Jeremy Akerman

Then there is "The Partisan", best typified by John Diefenbaker, who seems to be utterly blind to the virtues of anyone but himself and to any arguments but his own. Of course, nearly all politicians profess that the party to which they belong is superior to the opposition, but there are those who carry this to an extraordinary degree.

The members of this group are rarely able to see any merit in their opponents: if they are in government they dismiss opposition proposals as complete nonsense; if in opposition, they denounce all government plans as evil.

Some partisans, like Tory chief John Buchanan, give the impression that they really believe that the government is invariably bad and their party invariably good, but others fall into this group because they are essentially subscribers to the "adversary system" of politics. These latter are usually lawyers who carry the courtroom system into the Legislature, believing that they should fight for their side, right or wrong, and concede nothing to their opponents.

One of the most skilful practitioners of this art I have seen was former Premier G. I. Smith, who had an unparalleled ability to summon up great wrath and righteous indignation at the drop of a hat and, if you were not careful, could almost convince you that the people he was berating were the most heinous villains under the sun. Premier Gerald Regan is also possessed of this ability, but usually only uses it when his side is in trouble (when he has amazing skill in making weakness appear to be strength) or when his opponents are on the run and he cannot resist rubbing more salt into the wounds.

Some backbenchers, trying to ingratiate themselves with their party's leadership, also cast themselves as great partisans, but, generally speaking it is a role which lacks credibility and is relatively unprofitable.

Regan and Smith also fall into the next category, that of the "Orator". Good speakers are few and far between and the vast majority of members of legislatures and parliament are by no means orators of any standing. To qualify for this designation the member has to possess a voice which is loud and clear. He has to enunciate his words carefully, has to organize his speech in a logical and natural sequence of points, has to modulate his delivery to suit the nature of the various passages, and he has to make the speech persuasive and interesting.

No great speech can ever be read word for word (although this is done quite frequently) and a speech devoid of humour is not likely to get high marks unless it is on a matter of grave seriousness. A speech which is repetitive and rambles on over old ground or which contains too much chest thumping will not make the grade.

There are some members who have exceptional oratorical abilities, but who may not be consistent or who may introduce into their speeches elements which may mar an otherwise superb address. Others come in like a lion and go out like a lamb.

Jeremy Akerman

Orators are basically of two varieties: the serious or "old fashioned" kind and the "performers", whose speeches are great entertainment in addition to being informative and weighty. The former, "old fashioned" variety deliver their addresses in stately tones, with well constructed language, and appeal to lofty ideals and concepts. Smith, Diefenbaker and David Lewis are in this category. The performers, like Regan, Tommy Douglas and Dave Barrett, deliver wide-ranging, freewheeling, highly entertaining orations, peppered with jokes, laced with sarcasm, and replete with devastating attacks upon their opponents.

Both styles require certain talent and practice, but in order to qualify must hold the attention of the listener until the last word is spoken.

I think, perhaps, the finest parliamentary speech I have ever heard was delivered in the British House of Commons by the controversial Member of Parliament for South Down, Mr. Enoch Powell. Without the assistance of a single note, Powell unfolded the most convincing case against direct representation in the proposed European Assembly and did so with such controlled emotion and obvious conviction that it was a moving experience. I might add that Mr. Powell, who appeared to be ill at the time, delivered this speech without raising his voice, relying entirely on perfect construction, superb phrasing and sheer eloquence.

Perhaps it may be argued that it takes an issue of deep fundamental importance to the nation to bring

What Have You Done for Me Lately?

out this type of speech, but if that is the case we in Canada should be treated to dozens of great orations as we certainly are faced with several burning questions of lasting national consequence.

There are the "Funny Men" among elected members who may be superb wits, like former Tory MLA Jim MacLean, or poker-faced joke tellers like Liberal Ron Wallace, who can bring the House to its knees in helpless mirth. There are some, who shall be nameless, who do not intend to be amusing yet still provoke laughter, and others the content of whose speeches may not be particularly amusing, but whose mannerisms and form of delivery are designed to raise a smile.

Without the "Funny Men" the Legislature would be a very dull place.

There are "Opposition Men" who in government would not unduly inspire, yet who in opposition shine with a bright light. These are the members who are always ready to attack, always prepared to question, ever willing to laboriously examine the fine print.

Former Tory MLA Gerald Ritcey was of this type, fearless, well prepared and alert in opposition, yet irritable and defensive in government. There are the "Independents", like Harry How, whose reactions are spontaneous, emotional and unpredictable and, in many instances, unforeseen even by their own colleagues.

There are the "Fifty-one Percenters", who sit on the fence with their ears to the ground ready to espouse whatever cause or viewpoint they determine to be popular with a majority of the electorate at any given time.

There are the "Demagogues", who, right or wrong, tell people what they want to hear and can turn the obscure into the obvious, virtue into villainy, black into white, innocence into guilt.

There are the "Nightwatchmen", who are skilled in "holding things up" by being ever ready, without a shred of preparation, to be called upon to stall proceedings until the next day. Negative as this role at first appears, it can often be invaluable to a party leadership which wants to launch a serious offensive in a debate but is unprepared to do so because its speakers or material will not be available until a later time.

Tory MLA Roger Bacon is the perfect "Nightwatchman" and can be relied upon, when needed, to deliver a lengthy, provocative speech, saying virtually nothing, on any subject under the sun, thus gaining valuable time for his colleagues to gather their material and wits.

There is the "Heckler" who rarely enters open debate to deliver a speech, but is expert in interrupting and goading other speakers.

There is the "Quiet-but-effective" type who is seldom heard from, but whose supporters always claim is an outstanding constituency person and very effective behind the scenes—claims which in some cases are accurate, in others not.

The list could go on, but we will end with the

What Have You Done for Me Lately?

"Naturals" like Finance Minister Peter Nicholson and my colleague Buddy McEachern who are what they are, open, and with little artifice or pretension. It hardly needs saying that the "Naturals" are the most popular members of the House.

This, then, is the strange assortment of humanity which has been sent by the people to that place known as "The House".

Jeremy Akerman

4: The House

Strictly speaking the term "the House" in parliamentary terminology may be applied to the assembly room and its precincts, but when elected members use the term it is generally taken to mean the actual chamber in which the debates are conducted. These chambers vary greatly across Canada from the small, intimate legislatures of Prince Edward Island and Nova Scotia to rather grandiose affairs in Ontario and Quebec. The Manitoba chamber, for example, is set in a semi-circle with a high ceiling adorned by gold leaf and flying cherubs. The Nova Scotia legislature is to be found in an ancient but tiny old building which is lost amid the highrise modern bank and office buildings of downtown Halifax, while most others across the country are found in huge, elaborate structures surrounded by acres of lawns and flower beds. The House of Commons in Ottawa and London are located in imposing edifices and commanding positions in the landscape.

It has been to this grand and lofty ideal that the Legislatures of the central and western provinces have aspired, while Maritime legislatures have more in common with the cosy, unpretentious chambers

Jeremy Akerman

to be found tucked away in the sde streets of the Caribbean countries.

Before the House goes into session it looks immaculate. The plush carpets demand that the visitors lower their voices and the desks and microphones are clean and shiny. Once the members have been in it for an hour or two, the chamber takes on a very different appearance with books and papers over the desks and floor, wastebaskets overflowing, attache cases by the seats, and glasses of water—and the odd cup of coffee—very much in evidence.

This is, after all, a place of work. This is where the members will spend literally hundreds of hours listening, speaking, questioning, writing letters, studying legislation, reading reference books (and, sometimes, if the speaker is not eagle-eyed, the occasional newspaper) and generally trying, each in his or her own way, to represent their constituents.

The House is merely an inorganic structure, given a certain atmosphere by the historic architecture or the portraits of Charles Tupper and Henry Fielding on the walls, but it absorbs the collective condition of the members into its own personality. When there is a bitter controversy, the House is hostile and edgy; when the pressure is off (usually when the Premier is out of town and the affable Peter Nicholson is in charge), the House becomes co-operative, relaxed and amiable; towards the end of a wearying session the House is irritable and oppressive.

This may sound like so much fanciful nonsense, but this is what members mean when they talk

What Have You Done for Me Lately?

about "the mood" of the House. I have seen these many moods of the House from the helpless intoxication of a Ron Wallace laugh-in, the actual—and eminently forgettable—intoxication of a late night sitting, the stunned abhorrence of a physical assault by one member upon another, to the hostile and bitter turmoil precipitated by an outbreak in the gallery.

The mood of the House is a major factor in determining the kind of speeches which will be given on a particular day, the extent to which members may be able to bend the rules, and whether or not any real work will be accomplished. Physically, the Speaker is the most dominant person in the House, in reality, the Premier is, and his mood usually infects the House as a whole.

The Speaker is given the virtually impossible task of applying equally, without fear or favour, the rules of debate with total consistency, but often both he and the rules can only serve as a guide. The Speaker is supposed to be sacrosanct whose word is law, but he, too, is human and on many occasions the Speaker is influenced by the House's mood.

If the House is generally hostile towards a particular speaker or to a certain argument the Speaker is liable to be more stern, more snappy, more rigid. If the member having the floor is well liked or if the notion he is expressing is lighthearted or commands widespread approval, the Speaker will likely overlook breaches of the rules. In a similar fashion the Speaker cannot help but be influenced by the nature and status of certain individual members of the

House.

G. I. Smith—a skilful parliamentarian who knew how to break the rules as well as to apply them—who had over twenty-five years service in the House and was a former premier, could consequently get away with murder. A rookie member of a rather irascible temperament would get short shift from the Speaker if he attempted to take the same liberties. Irrepressible members like Regan and Buchanan who are willing to gamble often make up their own rules as they go along. The cautious, hesitant back bencher would usually stand little chance in any serious attempt to circumvent the rule book.

While all Speakers are politicians and all are subject to human weakness, some will be more adapted to the role than others. In some ways the Speaker is required to be a political eunuch, and if his temperament is to be impatient or partisan, then he is likely to get into some scrapes.

I have been able to watch four Speakers of the Nova Scotia House at close quarters. The best was Mr. Speaker Mitchell, whose patience, courtesy and soothing qualities annoyed me when I first entered the legislature, but which I now see as being exactly what was required. The worst was Mr. Speaker Fitzgerald, who was far too partisan and short-fused to be in the chair without fireworks erupting (although I must confess that Mr. Regan, who was then in Opposition, did his best to aggravate, and must have sorely tried whatever patience the Speaker possessed).

What Have You Done for Me Lately?

The Speaker has the deciding vote in the event of a tie, at which time he is supposed to give his reasons for his vote. I remember the drama of George Mitchell breaking a tie in favour of a controversial bill of mine, explaining, perfectly correctly (although to the chagrin of his government colleagues, I suspect), that he was voting in such a way as to provide further consideration of the measure at a future time. I also remember the hilarity which greeted the reason given by Mr. Speaker Connolly when he broke a tie in favour of the administration: "Because I think the government is doing a fine job!"

There are various kinds of measures with which the members have to deal, each being dealt with in a different manner. Bills—that is those measures which are proposed to become Acts (or law)—receive three "readings" and consideration in two committees.

As I have already explained, a "reading" of a bill is nothing of the kind, in the sense that the contents of the bill are not read aloud. First reading is when the bill is introduced at which time no debate of any kind takes place. Second reading is subject to a vote and is approved in principle. It is at this stage of the bill when the extensive debate takes place and, with the exception of the member who introduced the bill who may close debate, each member may speak only once and for not longer than an hour (these are Nova Scotia rules. At Ottawa and in other legislatures the rules vary greatly).

If the bill is approved on second reading it is to

committee, where the public may make representations in favour of, or in opposition to, the bill. If the committee approves it, the bill comes back into the House in its manifestation as Committee of the Whole House (that is with the Speaker and the Mace removed and with much more flexible rules of conduct), where it receives a detailed clause by clause examination.

Often this stage turns out to be a mere formality, each clause being passed with amazing rapidity (signalled by choruses of "carried!"), but it is also at this stage that the so-called "filibuster" can be carried out since, in Committee of the Whole, there is no limit to the number of times a member may speak.

Resolutions are usually (but not always) opposition instruments and call upon the House to resolve that it is of a certain opinion with respect to topical issues. There is only one stage for a resolution, when it is debated and voted upon. Increasingly, opposition resolutions are never even called for debate or vote by the government, whose majority naturally controls the business of the House.

House Orders (or "Orders for Returns" as they are called in other parliaments) are motions calling the government to produce certain information, reports or documents. If the House Orders are relating to routine or non-controversial matters they will be passed with little fuss; but many are opposed by the government, whose spokesmen invariably declare that the compilation of the Return (or answer) would be too costly or because the release of the ne-

What Have You Done for Me Lately?

cessary information "is not in the public interest".

In some cases this claim will have validity if the order relates to sensitive negotiations which are still proceeding, but often the "public interest" is to be equated with the interests of the government party which fears possible embarrassment if the desired information is supplied.

Information is also sought in the Question Period, when members (usually of the opposition parties) direct verbal inquiries to various ministers of the Crown, who may or may not choose to answer. At Ottawa there is a daily question period, but it is of a very short duration, and as many as fifty members may all be trying to catch the eye of the Speaker in order to be recognized. Most of them will be disappointed and will have to try to ask their question on a future day.

Many people often get indignant with their M.P. because he or she did not "ask a question in the House" on a matter which concerns them, but since they do not understand the procedure, do not realize that a member might conceivably try for weeks to ask his question and never be given the floor. In the Nova Scotia Legislature the members do not have such an excuse, for while there are only two question periods a week (Tuesdays and Thursdays), there is no time limit, and, occasionally, the question period has continued for almost four hours.

There are strict rules governing the kind of questions which may be asked and the manner in which they must be posed. Here again, certain members get away with murder, but for the majority the questions must be concise, must not be argumentative and must seek information which may reasonably be supposed to be within the immediate knowledge of the Minister to whom the inquiry is directed.

Some ministers give informative and straight-forward answers, leaving everybody satisfied, but others are apt to supply evasive, empty or mischievous replies which usually cause nothing but trouble and hard feelings. Premier Regan is a master at giving answers which say nothing, and he does so in a way which can be utterly infuriating. He pretends not to have heard the question, then affects to have misunderstood it, then either gives a one word answer or launches into an interminable rambling speech as often as not unconnected with the question.

As I indicated, ministers are not obliged to answer if they do not want to, but normally if a minister does not know the answer—or does not want to give it—he will "take it as notice", which means he will supply it at a later date. Questions taken as notice may never surface again and it is often suspected by opposition members that this is a tactic to avoid possible embarrassment which might be posed by supplementary questions.

The standard joke in parliamentary circles on this matter concerns the minister who is asked how he is feeling that particular day and replies that he will take it as notice and answer at a future time. Two of the funniest exchanges during the question period were directed to the same minister, who is known for his quiet humour and his habitual avoidance of ever providing an answer.

The first went something like this (I stress at this point I am not quoting from Hansard, but drawing on recollection):

"Will the Minister tell the House if the moose population is increasing or declining?"

"Mr. Speaker, I will ask the moose," came the minister's straight-faced reply.

On the other occasion the minister did not fare as well: "Will the minister indicate if the Forest Improvement committee is active?"

"Yes, it is, Mr. Speaker."

"Has the committee been holding regular meetings?"

"Yes, Mr. Speaker."

"Can the minister name the members of the committee?"

"No, but I will take it as notice."

"Can the minister name the chairman of the committee?"

"No, not right now. I'll check on it."

"Is the minister aware that under the provisions of the legislation he is the chairman of that committee?"

It has become common for members of the house to receive indignant complaints from school groups who have visited the legislature and have left appalled by what they saw. They protest that the members are ignorant, ill-mannered, unconscientious and that the House is a shambles and a disgrace. There are rare occasions when this kind of criticism might be warranted, but invariably it is totally undeserved and again springs from a lack of understanding of what is going on.

It is worth examining their criticisms in some detail since the same complaints will probably have come to the minds of numerous onlookers who have dropped into the public gallery for a short time.

They say (and I am looking at one such letter of complaint as I write) that a number of members are not in their seats. They say that various members get up and walk out while someone is speaking. They see a member reading a newspaper or a book and a few others huddled in whispered conversation which they say is rude and ignorant. They hear members catcalling or laughing at another member's remarks, which they say is disgraceful.

First, the members who are not in seats might conceivably be playing hooky, but it is more likely that several are at a committee meeting downstairs, two ministers are in Ottawa on government business, one has received a long distance telephone call, and another has an engagement in his or her constituency (possibly to attend a school function!). The members who walk out while someone else is speaking may also be going to take telephone calls or to see a constituent who has come to the lobby asking for them. They might be on their way to an important meeting, simply to get a quick cup of coffee, or to use the washroom. Since there is always

What Have You Done for Me Lately?

someone speaking whenever the House is in session it is impossible not to leave during a member's remarks.

The member reading a book or a newspaper might be looking for some references to include in a speech he intends to make when the present speaker has finished. The few members huddled in conversation may be trying to decide who will speak next for their party, how they will vote on the particular measure before the House, or conferring on a proposal for sitting hours or orders of business which has just been sent across by the government whip.

The heckling is the most difficult to explain to persons unfamiliar with the parliamentary process, as it obviously does appear rude and unnecessary. In defence of catcalling, I can only resort once more to my contention that politicians are human beings. If they have been sitting for many hours, are having to listen to a speech they have heard seven times before, or are incensed or amused by a particularly brazen or contentious claim by the speaker, they give voice to their feelings. The repartee in heckling is what prevents the House from becoming an undertaker's parlour and it invariably acts as a spur to better debate.

Sometimes it does get out of hand and may be really offensive (in which case the Speaker will step in), but generally it does no harm and is sometimes beneficial.

Another common complaint raised by visiting school groups is that the House is boring. I have to confess that it sometimes is excessively boring, and two members of the Nova Scotia House—one past and one present—have been known to fall asleep on such occasions. This complaint is usually heard when the visitors have witnessed consideration of the Estimates. This is a tedious, but utterly vital, procedure which is carried on in Committee of the Whole (and is called by the members "Supply"), when the government's projections of its departmental spending are examined in detail by the opposition members. This process is at the very heart of the British Parliamentary system, under which the elected members control the public purse strings.

Opposition members may not, under the rules, propose any measure which will spend public money—such measures can only come from a minister—but they can and should give a thorough examination of the government's spending plans and, if necessary, hold up the money until the appropriate minister tells them what he intends to do with it.

With the consideration of Estimates, bills, resolutions, House Orders, questions and numerous committee meetings, the members' time is consumed while the House is sitting. With extremely poor facilities and little secretarial assistance (only ministers and party leaders get proper offices and staff in Nova Scotia—an absolute disgrace in my opinion), the ordinary member also has to write and prepare his speeches, do his research and deal with his correspondence.

While the House is in session there is plenty to keep the member busy and, in the next chapter, we shall consider what he does when he returns to the constituency.

Jeremy Akerman

"ENTERTAINING THE TROOPS"
THE PREEM IN HIGH GEAR
NOT EASY TO CAPTURE – THE
QUICKNESS OF THE MOUTH
DECEIVES THE EYE.

5: The Constituency

Before leaving to return to his constituency our new member may have drawn up a report in which he has listed the topics which were considered during the session and how he spoke or voted on them. This report may have been sent to every home in the riding by householder mail (The MLA has to pay five cents a house for this, the federal M.P. gets his free), just to his strongest supporters, to the local press or to selected persons who he thinks would be most interested. As he is packing his bags he may feel quite pleased with himself: he made a few fairly good speeches, he raised several questions of importance to his constituency and he was a diligent attender at all of the committees to which he had been assigned by his party.

Because he may not fully trust the media to convey accurate reports back home he may also have sent press releases to the local paper and radio station stressing, in particular, that one special, critical problem which he feels is of top priority to his constituents. Let us say that problem is housing and our friend has repeatedly raised this matter at almost every available opportunity: he mentioned it in his speech on the Address in Reply to the Speech from the Throne; he directed it to the responsible minister during question period; he brought it up in committee, explained it in detail during the Estimates; and may have tabled a House Order seeking information on government programs connected with housing. He is, therefore, satisfied that, at least, on this one important subject he has done his very best to represent the people who sent him to the Assembly.

In their secret heart of hearts, all newly elected members probably harbour visions of being greeted by enthusiastic and appreciative crowds upon their return from their first session. It may occasionally happen to some member who has been the centre of a great controversy, but when our new member arrives at the airport or train station there is nobody to meet him—not even his wife who could not leave the kids. He saunters over to the news-stand to buy a paper and runs into the local clothing store owner, or president of one of the local unions. The greeting is hardly guaranteed to lift his spirits.

"Oh, Johnny! You're back. On vacation now, huh? Have a good time in Halifax?"

He smiles politely and mutters something about the real work only just beginning, but his friend continues: "What in the hell you fellas do down there anyway? You must have an easy time of it, I didn't hear nothing about you on the T.V. What a life! I wish I could get a paid holiday with tax free expenses!"

What Have You Done for Me Lately?

The taxi driver, a supporter, is more kind. He wants Johnny to know that he doesn't expect miracles.

"I was watching the news in case you'd be on, Johnny, but I guess you never got a chance to speak, huh? Well, never mind, you're only new and I guess it takes a while to learn the ropes."

When he gets home, after he hugs the kids, ignores his wife's question "have a nice time, dear?" and reads the paper, he telephones his campaign manager. At least he knows that Joe, his political right arm, will be informed, understanding and up on all the "talk" around town.

"Hi, Joe. It's me, Johnny."

"Johnny who?"

"'Johnny who?' For heavens' sake, the guy you elected to the Legislature, that's who!"

"Oh, Johnny! Sorry, boy, I wasn't thinking, I'm tied up with Ethel's family who are down from Toronto and the place is a madhouse. So what's new?"

"I was hoping you could tell me. What's all the talk around town? Anything about the session?"

"Things are pretty quiet. People don't expect too much of you yet, so you can coast for a while longer, but you're going to get a bit of flack about housing."

"Why?"

"Well, the least you could have done was to have mentioned it. Things are pretty desperate now y'know. Was talking to a couple of fellas very unhappy you never said anything about housing."

Jeremy Akerman

Johnny goes to bed extremely depressed, but since he now knows that politics is full of surprises, he feels that maybe tomorrow something good will happen.

Federal Members of Parliament are full time politicians, but in Nova Scotia the Members of the Legislature still carry on their business, profession or occupation. The Premier and cabinet ministers should be, and nearly all are, full time, but as of the time of writing only the NDP MLAs and one or two others devote their full time to their jobs as representatives. There has been considerable debate as to whether or not full-time representation is good or bad. Its opponents say that it tends to make the member narrow minded and one-tracked. The advocates say that the job of doing the people's business is so important and time consuming that the member has no business treating it as a hobby or sideline. I am, naturally, of the latter persuasion as I find there is not even sufficient time to get all the work done as it is, but there are interesting arguments on the other side.

One of the most powerful of those arguments is that in certain constituencies, there is not the demand for a full time member. Some rural members tell me that they have no problem whatever in coping with the problems of their constituents in the evenings and on weekends, and one member from the Halifax-Dartmouth metropolitan area told me he rarely receives more than six or seven calls a week from his constituents.

What Have You Done for Me Lately?

Frankly, I think this is mere rationalisation, as I believe the demand will increase in direct proportion to the degree of availability of the member. If people know that the member can be reached and welcomes their problems then they will go to him; if they know that the member is inaccessible they may not even try to contact him.

The reasons for many members not becoming full time may vary; they may be interested in politics but not that interested, they may enjoy their regular occupation too much to forsake it entirely, or, importantly, they may not want to forgo the income which they derive from two occupations. I receive my pay cheque every two weeks and it is, therefore, an eye-opener for me to see some members receiving their sessional indemnity (pay) in one big lump perhaps as much as four or five months from the start of the year, indicating that, at least until that point, their income from their regular occupation has been quite adequate to meet their needs.

Let us assume, for the sake of the argument, that our new member, Johnny, is a full time member. Let us also assume that he has a constituency office (which most do not) where he is available to meet the public and hear their problems and complaints. Since this represents my own situation and that of my party colleagues I can reconstruct from actual experience a day in the life of such a member when the house is not sitting.

7.30 a.m. The telephone. A man is leaving for work. He wants to know if he sends his wife down later in the day with a statutory declaration (an official form requiring an oath to be taken) will the member sign it? Is his wife making the declaration or is it the man himself? It is the man. No, he will have to come in himself in order for it to be legal. What time does he get off work? Four o'clock, but he has to go to a special union meeting so cannot be at his office until 5:30. The member explains that his office closes at 4:30 but he will wait until the man gets there.

The member plugs in the kettle to make coffee. The baby wakes up and has to be changed. With the wet baby under one arm he picks up the phone which is ringing again. It is a devoted party supporter who likes to chat. Did he hear the news? What news? On the radio, says the supporter, about the new lobster licensing regulations. No, explains the member, he hasn't had a chance to listen to the radio yet. The baby cries, the man gets the message and the conversation is terminated.

The kettle is boiling away like mad. The member makes coffee, turns on the radio to get "The World at Eight" and thinks about what he will have for breakfast.

The telephone. Will he be in his office today, a woman asks. Yes, says Johnny and tells her to come in around 3 o'clock.

He gets the frying pan and takes a few eggs out of the refrigerator, but before he proceeds any further he hears the news item referred to by his earlier caller and notes that his party is cited as having

What Have You Done for Me Lately?

taken a particular position. He calls one of his fellow MLAs. Does he know where the story came from? No, maybe from Fred. He calls Fred. Yes, says Fred, they phoned to ask for a comment, but it came out differently on the news. Call the radio station and correct it, Johnny tells him.

He cracks the eggs into the pan and butters some bread.

The telephone. A man he is due to represent before an appeal hearing wants to know at what time the hearing will be held. Johnny explains that his hearing is next month. Today's hearing is for Mrs. Jones whom he had forgotten until this moment. He calls Mrs. Jones to remind her to be there at eleven o'clock. Mrs. Jones says she has been ready since yesterday and is worried in case she doesn't win the case. Johnny says it is a tough one but they will do their best.

The eggs are hard and the coffee is cold.

Knock at the door. It is a young man who thinks the member is a soft touch and wants five dollars bus fare to go and apply for a job. Johnny, who knows the bus fare is only two dollars, gives him three.

The telephone. A woman thinks she has been underpaid by her employer and where can she lodge a complaint. He gives her the address and telephone number of the Department of Labour local office and tells her if she does not get satisfaction to call him back.

Johnny eats the eggs and makes a fresh cup of coffee.

Jeremy Akerman

The telephone. Yes, he will be in the office in the afternoon.

Joe calls. Has he remembered the meeting with the executive of the pensioners club at 9:30? Yes, he has and wants to ask Joe if—the baby has disconnected them.

He goes to the bathroom and starts to shave.

The telephone. What is the minimum wage, a woman asks.

$2.75 an hour, he says, but if she will call at the office around 2:30 he will check just to make a sure.

He finishes shaving and starts to dress for the day.

The telephone. No satisfaction at the Department of Labour says the woman, she could only get to speak with a secretary. What are the particulars, he asks? He scribbles the details on the corner of a page of *Maclean's* magazine. He will call her back later on.

He ties his tie, puts on his coat and decides to go down for the mail before the meeting.

As he is closing the door he hears the telephone ringing. A complicated pension case. Can the man come into the office and bring all the papers with him? The man does not sound pleased at this suggestion and asks Johnny to go to his house. No, says Johnny, come to the office, it will be better. The man grumbles about overpaid politicians. Johnny weakens. Is the man sick or disabled? If he is then Johnny will make a special effort. Well, the man says, he is "not feeling well". Johnny agrees to go to the house but cannot guarantee when that will be. Probably later this evening.

What Have You Done for Me Lately?

As he is opening his car door a neighbour passes. "Sleeping late again, Johnny? What a life!"

The pensioners' club wants to build an extension to their hall, but don't have the money. What will it cost? Maybe as much as $15,000 they think. Can Johnny get a grant from the government? Johnny opines that he might be able to get $8,000 or even $10,000 if lucky, but that the pensioners will have to raise the rest locally. They discuss possible methods of getting the money. Johnny makes a donation of $50 to start the ball rolling.

After the meeting has broken up one of the pensioners detains Johnny by the door. He did not get the Supplement to his old age pension this month. Will Johnny call Halifax for him? Sure, says Johnny, but will the pensioner phone him at the office in the afternoon to remind him?

Johnny is late for the appeal hearing and drives like the wind, casting his eyes about for RCMP patrols. He arrives ten minutes after Mrs. Jones' case is supposed to commence. Mrs. Jones, who is sitting in the waiting room, tells him a man came out and informed her they were running behind time and that her case might not be heard until eleven-thirty.

He goes through the case with her once more. It is a tricky workmen's compensation matter. Mrs. Jones is claiming a pension because she feels her husband died as a result of the disease for which he was being compensated. Her family doctor is unequivocal that Mr. Jones' death was caused by his disease, but the specialists in Halifax say it was a heart attack.

Jeremy Akerman

Johnny has to tie the two together and has brought some medical books with him. He does not think the case can be won and tries to prepare her for that eventuality.

The hearing goes better than expected and Johnny is now mildly optimistic about the outcome which will be communicated by mail in a few weeks.

His office hours begin at one o'clock and when member arrives at 1:15 there are seven people in the waiting room. This is where his real, eyeball to eyeball work begins and where, for the next three or four hours, he will listen to as many as thirty hard luck stories ranging from minor nuisances to utter misery. Interspersed between these personal talks with his constituents, he will receive and make as many phone calls.

Today there are twenty-two visitors to the office and fourteen incoming telephone calls. Of the personal visitations, two are regulars or "repeaters" who come to Johnny for advice on every domestic matter from coping with the eldest daughter who is "growing up too fast" to fetching in a bucket of coal. These are almost like old friends to the member as he sees them so often and he is kind, chatty, but firm about them doing some things for themselves.

One is a "speechmaker", that is, a person who has genuine problems but knows in advance that Johnny will be unable to solve them and has come to deliver a diatribe against the world and against politicians in particular. He takes up a full twenty minutes and when Johnny shows a little impatience becomes bel-

What Have You Done for Me Lately?

ligerent and stalks out of the office threatening to call the radio "talk show".

Two are housing problems; one a dispute with the landlord who is refusing to fix the leaking roof; the other a couple who are living in a car and want to get into public housing. Johnny undertakes to refer the first case to the Residential Tenancies Board, and to write a recommendation to the Housing Authority for the second.

Three cases are Social Assistance matters: one a widow whose daughter has become eighteen and whose cheque has been reduced as a result; a man whose doctor says he cannot work again and wants disability pension; the third, a mother a whose husband has deserted her, wants an increase in her cheque due to high drug costs connected with her baby's illness.

Discovering that the eighteen year old daughter of the first intends to continue in school, Johnny says he will call Halifax and straighten it out. The second man, he says, will receive official application forms in the mail within ten days. The white form is to go to the doctor, Johnny tells him, and the green one to be brought back to Johnny who will help fill it out. On the third case he will write to the Directors to see if a "special needs" allowance can be granted.

Two cases are unemployment insurance problems where confusion has resulted from incorrectly filed report cards or from clerical errors. Calls to the U.I.C. office bring promises of correction.

Two more are Old Age pension cases where the

recipients have not received their Guaranteed Income Supplement. Johnny discovers they were late in filing their annual application and explains that he will try to speed it up.

Three constituents, all young, are looking for work. They have been out of work for months, one since he left school a year earlier. They clearly convey the impression that they believe Johnny has a bag full of jobs under his desk and, when he explains that the best he can do is write them a reference, they are crestfallen.

Johnny is depressed. The unemployment rate in his area is over twenty per cent. He needs a cup of coffee.

Next comes a man whose driver's licence has been suspended for six months as a result of an impairment conviction. When Johnny says there is no power on earth or in heaven that can get his licence back, he is unhappy and says he heard those things could "be fixed".

Here is a woman whose family is embroiled in an emotional and complex battle over the will of a deceased relative. This is a long case and while Johnny stresses he is not a lawyer, he offers some advice as to how she should proceed.

Next, an unmarried mother with a tale of total misery. Her father has put her out of his home virtually without a stitch of clothing. She is unemployed, has been turned down by the municipal welfare office (telling her she should have thought of that when "she had a good time"), is temporarily living

What Have You Done for Me Lately?

with a friend who has loaned her clothes, and is now weeping uncontrollably.

Johnny starts calling various agencies and clergymen and manages to arrange a temporary solution. As soon as they can find a place for her to live, Johnny says he can get her Social Assistance. She tells Johnny she will work for him in the next election.

Four workmen's compensation cases have also emerged this afternoon: one for whom the board has refused to supply drugs related to the compensable condition; a second who has been ordered back to work by the board despite the fact that the man's doctor says he cannot return for at least three more weeks; the third who has been receiving benefits for three years has suddenly been informed that they will be reduced due to new medical evidence; the fourth who was injured in the mine many weeks ago and despite the correct reports having been filed still has not received any payment.

Johnny makes the appropriate notes to write the board and tells the men he will contact them as soon as he receives a reply.

The man with the statutory declaration does not show up even though Johnny waits until 5:45.

During and between these visitations the member has taken the telephone calls. Three seeking information on various pieces of legislation or regulation; one to set an appointment for the following day, two return calls from government departments in Halifax, three to complain that various cheques were late this month, two complaints about the municipal garbage disposal, one long-winded woman giving an interesting but exotic suggestion on how the taxation system should be re-arranged, and one call from the press who wants Johnny's reaction to a newly announced government program.

At the busiest time of the afternoon an old, but friendly pensioner called "just to pass the time of day," wanting to chat about "how the party is doing these days."

During supper, the telephone rings twice and Johnny answers, his mouth full. Joe wanting to know if he met with the pensioners and how it turned out. A woman, with a strangely familiar voice, asking about the Department of Labour.

Johnny apologises for having forgotten about her problem and, being unable to locate the *Maclean's* magazine on which he wrote his notes, once again takes down the details. Tomorrow morning, he promises her, she will have an answer.

The telephone rings again, but Johnny's wife absolutely refuses to allow him to answer.

After supper Johnny has to attend a meeting of the mineworkers' union. Here he is questioned on mine safety regulations, workmen's compensation and the imposition of a new sales tax. He receives a vote of thanks and chats with the miners after the meeting, picking up three new cases in the course of so doing.

Just as he is about to accept an invitation from one of them to go to have a beer, he remembers the pen-

What Have You Done for Me Lately?

sion case of the man who is too ill to leave his house. He regretfully declines the kind invitation and drives to the other side of town, where he is greeted by the man, in perfect health, who grumbles about "some people coming at all hours of the day and night."

Home again, Johnny watches the late news on T.V., takes one more call from a man who knew he was still up because he saw the lights on, checks his notebook (a party rally the next night and a school graduation the night after that), and goes to bed.

At 1:30 the telephone rings and the baby wakes up. The caller tells him that "a couple of the boys" are having a drink and want Johnny to settle an argument they are having What year did Mackenzie King become Prime Minister? Johnny says he doesn't know and, what is more, he doesn't care.

The man informs his member that that is the last time he is going to vote for somebody who is "stuck up" and hangs up.

Johnny crawls back to bed. The baby is still crying.

Jeremy Akerman

"THE NIGHTWATCHMAN"
ROGER BACON IN A MEAN MOOD

6: The Leader

There are few politicians who do not, at one time or another, secretly aspire to be leader of their party. Even those who may fully realize that they do not possess the natural talents for leadership, occasionally spare a fleeting daydream of being called upon, as the compromise statesmanlike candidate, to take the helm in time of crisis. This seldom, if ever, happens and the way to the so-called top is rough. Staying there can be even rougher.

If you can accept the argument that, basically, people do not do things they really hate, you can accept the notion that the party leaders are always there because they love it. This is not always true. There are innumerable instances of leaders staying in office long enough after they have lost the zest for the position, long after their health may have failed, long after they have yearned to return to the ease and privacy of the average citizen. Such leaders may hang on because they have been prevailed upon by party stalwarts not to leave the ship in its hour of need, because they may be terrified of what their most likely successors might do, or because—while they may be tired and ready to retire - "the job is still not finished".

Jeremy Akerman

I am not suggesting that all party leaders live in misery, but I cannot avoid the feeling that having jockeyed and battled for the top job, once they have experienced its rocky road often wish they could be backbench members again.

The leadership of a political party is no picnic. In addition to the work and frustrations of the ordinary elected member the leader has extra burdens and responsibilities, far more telephone calls, infinitely more mail, many more evenings away from home and greater pressures upon him. He has to worry about, not one, but all constituencies, solve problems for not only his voters, but everybody's voters, be available not only for organizations in his own district but all over the province. While he may receive a little undeserved praise for his party's successes, he will most assuredly receive the condemnation for its failures. He is expected to show strong leadership, but not "interfere" or unduly influence the party. He is supposed to keep everybody happy yet not be "a phony."

If he has a high profile he is a "headline hunter" and is building a cult of personality. If he espouses popular causes he is an opportunist, if he goes his own way he is arrogant and aloof. Spending a deal of time on his papers and research, he faces the accusation that he does not have the common touch and will not mingle with the masses; devoting much time to travelling and talking to people. he will be called shallow.

On making an effort to deal with and raise the

What Have You Done for Me Lately?

minor but important problems submitted by local people he finds himself charged with missing the "critical" issues of the day; on concentrating on matters of a general nature he finds he has neglected the "bread and butter" issues.

When he fails to appear at social events he is "snobby"; when he does he is asked who is doing his work while he's having fun.

The party leader who is also Premier or head of government has an even tougher time of it. His schedule is gruelling, meeting running into meeting, problem running into problem, request piling on request. His volume of calls and letters is such that he cannot possibly attend to more than a fraction himself and has to delegate to his staff. When a controversial issue is rampant in the land his mail might conceivably run into the thousands and his telephones be perpetually ringing. He has to negotiate with other governments and prospective industries, preside over the cabinet, ride herd on his ministers (restraining the more ebullient ones, prodding the lethargic ones), meet with delegations of mayors, union leaders, business organizations, charitable societies. In his spare moments he has to eat a thousand dinners at a thousand public banquets, speak to hundreds of meetings—party and otherwise—and keep his own party members from rebellion.

This latter task may not be easy. From the moment he selects his first cabinet he has made enemies within his own party, for everyone who has been excluded from that select and honoured group has harboured hopes of getting in and will be bitterly disappointed when he does not. He may have had to succumb to the claims of seniority and service to the party at the expense of rejecting a brighter, more promising talent. He may be asked to overrule a cabinet minister who has rejected a backbencher's request for a hundred miles of paving.

Some backbenchers will relate horror stories of offended voters in their area because the government is moving "too fast" in social legislation. Others will express impatience that the administration has not yet ushered in Utopia.

Subjected to these conflicting forces and to ever increasing pressures, it is small wonder that some heads of government retreat behind the wall of personal assistants and end up, like Richard Nixon, dealing with paper instead of people.

The size of the boss's personal staff varies greatly from place to place and we have all heard reports of the apparently ever-increasing size of Prime Minister Pierre Trudeau's personal entourage, which is now supposedly over a hundred. In Nova Scotia, the Premier has three main assistants, a personal private secretary and about six or seven other people who perform a variety of functions. He can, of course, draw upon the services of other staff elsewhere if he needs them. The Leader of the Opposition has a staff of about five, while I have a two—a secretary and an assistant.

In order to qualify for this assistance the party of the Recognized Leader, as he is called, must have at

What Have You Done for Me Lately?

least two members in the house, have run candidates in more than half the constituencies and received 10% or more of the total popular vote. The legislation governing this matter is somewhat strange because, presumably, if there was no third party at any particular time the Leader of the Opposition would still qualify for his staff even if he was the lone representative of his party.

Once the party leader has been chosen, he is not necessarily there for good. In Canadian politics the leader is chosen at conventions representative of the party membership as a whole, but in Britain he or she is selected by the Members of Parliament from among their own ranks. A leader who is also head of a government is likely to be secure in his position, but one in opposition—particularly if he has led the party through a couple of unsuccessful elections—may be looking over his shoulder at those who are waiting for the right moment to bid for his job.

In the Liberal and Conservative parties deposing an incumbent leader is a tricky and messy business since the mechanism to oust him is either obscure or non-existent. In the New Democratic Party the mechanism is built into the party constitution and, in theory, anyone may oppose the leader at the party's conventions held every second year. NDP Leaders, therefore, cease to exist at the start of the convention and have to account for their stewardship and seek re-election at the end of the convention.

The difference in parties also results in a some-

Jeremy Akerman

what different kind of leadership in each and varying degrees of authority which the party grants to the leader. Obviously, a leader who is head of government will be able to wield immense authority over the party for even if the prestige of his office and his control of important appointments does not bring a rebellious party in line, he still possesses the enormously powerful threat of resignation.

In some political parties the leader is not only the chief political spokesman but also head of administration and organization, in so far as he is entitled to appoint all party staff and therefore effectively control all internal party affairs. In the New Democratic Party these matters are directed by the elected executive and council of the party (which also makes all party appointments) and any leader who attempts, no matter how correctly, to unduly influence the direction of these affairs is likely to be resented.

The amount and nature of the work done by a party leader will depend to a great extent on the kind of person he is. Some take very few telephone calls and do not answer all correspondence. I have established a firm policy of answering every letter (except anonymous ones and the surprising number which bear no return address) as I feel that if a person has taken the trouble to write I should find the time to reply even if my reply may not be the one the person wishes to receive. I estimate that in the course of a year my staff and I will deal with about 5,000 individual problems and complaints (some of which may be from "repeaters"—persons with more than one problem) and receive and reply to approximately 3,000 letters. The number of telephone calls is impossible to estimate with even the remotest degree of accuracy.

The life of a party leader, therefore, can be exhilarating and rewarding, but very demanding and extremely exhausting. Some could not live without the dangers and excitement of leadership, others are reluctant and grudging, but they all know that while they are first to get the spotlight, they are the first to get the blame.

Jeremy Akerman

"THE AFFABLE NICHOLSON"
IS HE REALLY LISTENING
OR THINKING OF SCOT JOPLIN?

7: Private Conscience, Public Will and the Party Line

Frequently, one hears the complaint that elected members too often "toe the party line" instead of saying what they really think. This is an extremely common cry, yet, at the same time on certain types of issues (like capital punishment) the same people will criticize the members for voting according to their consciences instead of following popular opinion.

To what extent, and under what circumstances should the politician follow his inner voice and when should he allow himself to become a mouthpiece of the party or public?

Under the present parliamentary system in Canada where elections are contested along party lines and upon party "platforms", the administration, or government, is formed by the party securing the largest number of seats in the assembly (unless that number was an actual minority of the total number of seats and the other parties formed a coalition). This being the case, party discipline is important, especially for the governing party. Clearly, no government could survive very long if significant numbers of its own members consistently voted against important government legislation.

It is important to a lesser extent to an opposition party, but while in opposition the party can afford the luxury of allowing its members more freedom than it would were it in power, the party will be wary about letting it get out of hand lest the impression be created the party is an uncoordinated, poorly-lead team.

Consequently, the individual feelings and opinions of members will often have to be made subservient to the "party line" and if the member has failed to convince a majority of his colleagues in caucus (the term generally used to describe the elected members of a particular party) of the wisdom of his opinion, he must then go along with the caucus unless he wishes to be regarded as disloyal to his colleagues. This happens with more frequency than perhaps the public suspects, as the larger the number of members in a given party caucus the greater likelihood of there never being unanimity on most issues.

Therefore, in many cases, the member's fight to have his ideas adopted takes place not in the legislature or parliament, but in the caucus. This is especially true for government members, as the public and the media attach greater adverse significance to a member rebelling against his party if it is in power than when it is in opposition. This factor assumes even more important proportions if there is a narrow margin between the number of seats held by the

What Have You Done for Me Lately?

government and the number held by the combined opposition parties, for if the government loses its majority on a crucial measure—such as a budget—it is out of office.

(It is debatable as to precisely what measures constitute questions of "confidence" on which the government stands or falls, but it is generally accepted that a major piece of legislation and certainly a budget or a tax is a matter on which the government must secure a majority of votes in the house if it is to continue to govern).

Let us return, for a moment, to Johnny our newly elected member. Let us suppose that Johnny is fiercely opposed to increasing the sales tax, but that the leadership of his party has placed just such a suggestion before the party caucus. The leadership will outline its position and will recommend that the caucus officially adopt the proposal.

Along with other caucus members Johnny will get up and speak his piece, outlining his reasons for not agreeing with the leadership—possibly becoming quite heated or eloquent in his remarks. Since the caucus meeting is strictly private, the public will not hear this, and unless somebody "tells tales", will never even know about it.

Johnny does his best, wheels out all his arguments, appeals to reason, then to emotion, but is unsuccessful. The vote is taken and a majority of the caucus decides it will officially espouse the raising of the sales tax. What can Johnny do now?

Under the American system, Johnny would have

little trouble. There the party labels mean far less and the party line is usually non-existent or hard to define, Southern Democrats voting with Northern Republicans and vice versa. But in the Canadian and British system Johnny has a problem. The stance he now takes depends largely upon how strongly he feels on the issue and his sense of obligation and loyalty to the party.

If he wants to be considered a "good party man" and a "good loser", he will go into the house with his colleagues and will vote for the increase in sales tax and possibly even speak in favour, rationalizing that the greater good of the party is more important than his own personal feeling. If he does not wish to be disloyal to the party, but cannot bring himself to vote for something he believes to be wrong, he may absent himself from the house at the time of the vote. If he feels that to leave the house at such a critical time would be wrong, or if he wants the public to know his position on the issue, he may speak briefly, pointing out that while he has the highest regard for the leader and for his colleagues and while he recognizes that they have made many telling points, he has reluctantly to follow his own conviction and vote with the other side.

Finally, if Johnny considers the increase in sales tax to be an issue utterly critical to the nation and so completely alien to his political philosophy and personal morality, he may resign from his party, from his seat in the house, or both.

Since very few issues will be as monumental as to

What Have You Done for Me Lately?

prompt this last course of action it happens most infrequently and, in most cases where a member finds himself in disagreement with the party, he will say nothing and vote with his colleagues (in my experience, with government members, this almost always happens).

Many readers will have found the foregoing distasteful and will have come to the conclusion that Johnny and others like him are mere tools of the party. This would be an unfair judgment as they should realize that, if the parliamentary system of party government is not to dissolve in total shambles, a reasonable degree of party discipline simply has to be maintained. If such discipline disappeared, governments would be in and out of office every second day, and, ultimately, a congressional-type assembly of independents would demand that the executive, or government, be determined by a presidential system.

Notwithstanding this point, the reader is entitled to ask if it has to be that strict, if the system has to deny Johnny a greater opportunity to take his own positions.

The answer, in my opinion, is no. It does not have to be that rigid and we could definitely give the elected members more scope to express their individual feelings. Provided we did not go too far, I feel it would be most beneficial. One of my first actions in the Nova Scotia Legislature was to introduce a bill to create just such opportunities for ordinary members by having it stated in law that the government could

Jeremy Akerman

only fall if it were defeated on an issue which they had previously indicated was one which they considered a matter of confidence in the administration. The bill was defeated with both Liberals and Conservatives voting against it on the grounds, if I remember correctly, that it would usher in the United States system.

On that very bill I got the strong impression that a number of members who voted it down did not really disagree with its intent because it did not propose anything very startling or revolutionary. Since that time, two members of the house in particular Harry How and myself have advocated changes in the direction first indicated by that bill.

Consider the literally hundreds of measures, bills and resolutions, whether introduced by government or opposition back-benchers, which were not primarily of a partisan nature on which stimulating and enlightening debates could have occurred had members been free of the party whip. Obviously, matters of an ideological nature or questions firmly established in party policy together with major government proposals would have to be subject to party discipline, but so-called "free" votes could be held on many items and would introduce a new and invigorating element into the house. At the present time such "free votes" are very few and far between and even when they do occur they do not seem to be as free as one might suppose.

A case in point would be a bill introduced by an opposition member dealing with a relatively innocuous subject, but generally effecting a beneficial change. The mentality of our government is such that they cannot allow any opposition measure to pass simply, it would appear, because it comes from the opposition and usurps what the administration considers its Divine right to initiate legislation.

In such an instance two curious phenomena may be observed. The first is the excruciating experience of various government spokesmen (whom one suspects very strongly are not really opposed to the bill at all) twisting themselves inside out to demonstrate why the bill is useless or drawing absurd analogies to discredit it (when I proposed a bill to remove the disqualification from persons with previous criminal convictions running for municipal office, it was suggested that I wished to stock to capacity every town and county council with murderers and rapists).

The second phenomenon is that while some government members vote for the proposed opposition member's bill, there always seems to be a majority of them who ensure its defeat. The opposition member whose bill has thus been given the boot will, perhaps, be forgiven if he harbours suspicions that the thing has been "fixed".

The point is, of course, that there are members on all sides of the house with valid and interesting views on a variety of matters who would be far more creative and effective giving expression to what they really feel than in delivering a contrived spiel which has been designed to justify a prearranged party position. Some of the best speeches I have heard have been given by members who spoke from the heart, free of the party whip, and I think history records that some of the most memorable perorations of all time were given under similar circumstances.

It is interesting to draw a comparison between Canadian Parliaments and the British House of Commons, where a tradition has been firmly established by such towering figures as Randolph Churchill, Joseph Chamberlain and Ni Bevan of speaking out—often vociferously—against one's own party and colleagues. True, there are not many Bevans and Chamberlains in British politics today, but a Canadian observer would be amazed by the latitude which is enjoyed by M.P.s, particularly back-benchers, who are frequently to be heard roundly denouncing their own parties and trading quite vicious insults with their own colleagues on the floor of the House.

In Canada the party line is much more rigid, especially in cases like Peter Lougheed's almost paranoid concept of "team" government, and the ordinary Member is not expected to voice any more than a mild objection to a policy decided upon by his colleagues. What is commonplace at Westminster is rarely tolerated here, and readers may draw their own conclusions as to which country has suffered as a result of which practise.

The difference, I feel, is that in Canadian politics virtually every word a member says is filed away in his record to be used in judging him at a later time, whereas in Britain what counts is how the member votes in the division lobbies on those matters which are of central importance to the party and which the party leadership has declared to be a serious question of confidence.

The discussion on the conflict between the member's own opinion and the party line concerns what I can best term the "policy" issues. When it comes to the "lifestyle" or moral issues (which I believe should be, and usually are, free votes), the conflict is of a different kind. Here we are speaking of issues like abortion and capital punishment where, regardless of ideology and party, members will have deeply held passionate convictions which they cannot subject to the normal caucus decision making process.

Here the conflict is whether the member should vote according to his own conscience or whether he should vote the way the public wants him to vote. This is indeed a difficult dilemma: if he does not he stands accused of being anti-democratic and "flying in the face" of the public will.

The best example of this kind of dilemma is the great capital punishment debate in June of 1976, when on second reading of a bill the members voted (by a majority of eight) to abolish capital punishment while the popular opinion polls were indicating that as high as 75% of the Canadian people favoured its retention.

Many citizens who favoured retention were outraged that their Members of Parliament voted for abolition. They claimed that their M.P.s had ceased to represent them, were flouting the will of the people, had not "asked them" for their opinions and, consequently, demanded that the whole question be put to a referendum.

Ignoring the question as to whether these people would have demanded a referendum had the polls indicated a majority for abolition, it is important to note that the idea of submitting issues to referenda is basically alien to the British Parliamentary system of representation, since it negates the whole purpose of electing a parliament.

New Brunswick Conservative M.P. Gordon Fairweather has drawn the distinction between a "representative" and a "delegate". He says that delegates like those going from a particular state to a United States presidential nominating convention, for example are sent by their people with specific instructions to vote a specific way and are bound by those instructions. In contrast, he says, are members elected under our parliamentary system who are representatives chosen by the people for their capabilities and, apart from being expected to stick with the platform on which they campaigned, to exercise their own judgment based upon the evidence which is available to them but to which the public does not always have access.

This notion is not original and is held to have been first propounded by the famous English parliamentarian Edmund Burke, who went even further to intimate that he didn't care too much what his constituents thought about anything.

Even if the member has asked his constituents for their opinion and has ascertained by talking to every

What Have You Done for Me Lately?

single one of them (clearly an impossibility) that an overwhelming majority hold views contrary to his own, he is still faced with the same basic dilemma on one of these moral or "lifestyle" issues. Should he say that, regardless of his own deep convictions, he will have to vote the way the majority of his constituents want him to; or should he say that he cannot sacrifice his conscience and personal integrity in order to keep on the right side of public opinion?

It is a question each person has to answer in his own way. Personally, I agree with Mr. Fairweather on an issue such as this and that, whether I agree with my M.P. or not, he should vote according to his conscience. I say that because it seems to me that if he does not stick with his own conviction he is likely to be a man who will shift and change as public opinion changes.

In other words, if my Member of Parliament cannot be true to himself, how can he be true to anyone else?

Jeremy Akerman

8: The Power of the Press

Electing a government is not quite as simple as merely sitting down, looking over the alternatives and deciding which is the best. What needs to be considered are the factors which help the voters reach their decision. There are many such influences: money (which we shall discuss in the next chapter), calibre of candidate, style of campaign, and the power of the press.

In the middle of the last century Joseph Howe waged his famous battle for the freedom of the press and it is an interesting exercise to speculate on what old Joe Howe would think if he could come back and take a look at the "free" press he helped to create.

The ideal notion is that the voters will be able to make a reasoned decision based upon truthful information which is provided to them by the media without fear or favour. It simply does not happen that way. Nobody denies the perfect right of a newspaper, for instance, to print whatever editorial comment it pleases on any subject; but in its selection of what is printed as news, the way in which that news is written and the manner in which it is displayed in the paper can exercise a degree of control over the way in which information is digested by the public. Consequently, they can have a pronounced influence over the political decision making process.

Examples are easy to cite. For instance, if a newspaper favours a particular party or politician they may print every single item issued by that party, whether or not those items are really newsworthy. Conversely, if the paper dislikes a particular party they will make sure that many of its press releases and public statements are either not carried at all or are "buried" on a back page underneath the molasses advertisement.

Those items which are printed can be given a false sense of importance by the headline, the actual writing of the story and its placement in the paper. Mr. Jones, leader of the party to which the newspaper is favourable, may make a very weak statement requesting the government to consider an aspect of the fishing industry. If the story is carried on page one under a screaming red banner headline "JONES BATTLES FOR FISHERMEN'S RIGHTS", the public is likely to get the impression that Jones is indeed the on-going champion of fishermen.

Mr. Smith, leader of a party which the paper does not like, may have been conducting a genuine fight for the fishermen over a period of time and, in the latest of his attempts to secure justice, may have been unsuccessful in convincing the government to take action. If this story is carried on page 32 of the paper under a tiny headline: "Government rejects proposal", the public is not likely to receive a very strong impression of poor Smith's efforts.

This poor impression may be further accentuated if the story is written as if the government's rejection is the real news and tags on to the end of the story: "the government's position was outlined after Mr. Smith had spoken." Whether the public realizes it or not, this kind of thing is going on every day of the week.

Another tactic of the biased press might be in its reporting of the Legislature's question period. Let us suppose that Smith has been hammering the Minister of Fisheries in a series of well-constructed questions on a matter of importance, to which the Minister responds that action will be taken. On a supplementary question Jones gets into the act by asking the Minister to clarify that something will definitely be done. The Minister again says that it will.

The headline the next day reads: "MINISTER TELLS JONES GOVERNMENT WILL ACT." Poor Smith's name may not even be mentioned.

Similar mischief is perpetrated in the style of writing and by the insertion of subjective descriptions of what actually happened. Jones, the paper's favourite, addresses a meeting of 60 people. The report is as follows (italicized are the words inserted to create a good impression):

> In a *peppery and well received* speech, last night, Mr. Jones told a *large and enthusiastic* crowd that the government had failed to meet the needs of the people. The speech, *which*

> *was interrupted by applause*, systematically took the administration to task in a *devastating* series of examples of government incompetence.

On the same night, Smith, the man the paper does not like, addresses another meeting, also of 60 people (italicized are the insertions designed to create a bad impression):

> In a *rambling, philosophical tirade*, Mr. Smith told a *sparsely attended* meeting *of party faithful* that the government was not doing its job. His *lengthy* address, which was punctuated by *disturbances from the floor, attempted to show* how the administration had been incompetent.

(This latter example, incidentally, is taken from an actual newspaper story of a meeting addressed by Tommy Douglas in Cape Breton).

Thus what are "crowds" for the favourite is merely an "audience" for the man who is disliked. For Jones, they may be "masses of people", but for Smith, a "handful of party faithful". Jones "states"; Smith "mouths". Jones' candidates at election time are "standard bearers"; Smith's candidates "carry the banner". Jones releases his party's "platform"; Smith "unveils his manifesto."

The best (or worst) example of this kind of journalism must surely be the report of a meeting to

What Have You Done for Me Lately?

which I spoke in Antigonish during the 1970 election campaign. The story read:

> Mr. Akerman, whose expensive imported English tweed suit contrasted sharply with the plain garb of his tiny audience, said the NDP was the party of the little guy.

In case you are wondering, the suit in question was bought off the peg in a Sydney store for about $100. I searched the same paper very carefully to see if "Mr. Smith, in his old fashioned pinstriped banker's outfit, said the Tories are the party of the rich," but was unsuccessful in finding such a story!

The electronic media, radio and T.V. have a much greater excuse for offending a politician since they simply cannot cram every item into a five minute newscast and therefore must exercise a policy of rigid selection. Strange it is, then, that, generally speaking, radio and television are far more responsible and infinitely fairer than some newspapers. which do not have the same kind of restrictions imposed upon them.

Even in radio and television there are opportunities for undue bias, for instance, in the way questions are posed when the politician is being interviewed. Around about the same point in time both Smith and Jones have raised a particular issue.

The interviewer leads off on Jones with, "Mr. Jones, you're really going after the government on this issue; why do you feel it's important?"

This gives Jones the ideal opening to say that the issue is one of the most critical in the history of the world and that unless something is done the country will be brought to its knees.

Smith's question starts, "Mr. Smith, why are you jumping on Mr. Jones' bandwagon and what is all this stuff anyway?"

Smith, if he has time, first has to deny that he's jumping on anyone's bandwagon and that "all this stuff" is rather serious before he can start to make any real points. The idea, of course, is that Smith should not be able to make points!

Just as I have suggested that, perhaps, the public is often unfair and irrational in its criticism of politicians, so, I expect, will members of the news media feel I am being equally unfair and irrational. Let us therefore concede that it is true that a politician is never satisfied with the press coverage he receives and it is equally true that politicians are hypersensitive in their reactions to the media.

However, I firmly believe that I a have not greatly exaggerated the kinds of reporting and journalism which do occur from time to time and that a group of professionals who set themselves in judgment over the elected representatives so often should be prepared to have a look at their own house once in a while. At the very least, since they are so good in dishing it out, they should be ready to sit on the receiving end.

The fact of the matter is that all politicians do not get equal treatment from the media commensurate

What Have You Done for Me Lately?

with the importance of their statements and actions. There are some members who get excellent reporting no matter what they say or do; others could not buy it for love or money. The fact is that the media do "build up" certain politicians and in some cases "create" them, as happened, in my view, with Pierre Trudeau in 1968. It is equally fair to say, I think, that in other cases the media have "destroyed" politicians or, at least, have attempted to downgrade them such as occurred in Britain with Lord George Brown.

I have known many journalists and reporters both from my own experience in broadcasting and later in politics: some have been excellent, some terrible, some lazy, some diligent. While it is extremely dangerous to mention names, I must indicate that there have been two who have stood out for consistent hard work, solid journalism and scrupulous fairness.

They may not be Woodward and Bernstein, but Dan Page of CJCH and Mark Colpitts, formerly of CHNS, have impressed me as the kind of journalists whose numbers we could well afford to see increase.

It should further be said, perhaps, that no matter how hard a journalist tries to be objective, complete objectivity is neither possible nor even desirable. Since journalists are therefore no less human than politicians and since the people for whom they work have their own special interests and points of view, it is vital that the public fully realize the extent to which the media do influence their decisions.

While you think that the papers are, in the words of the old expression, printing "all the news that's fit to print", it is as well to remember that they decide what qualifies as being "fit".

9: Policy, Patronage and Cash

Before summing up the benefits and disadvantages of the life of a politician, a few words should be said about the formulation of party policy, the financing of political parties and the controversial question of patronage.

The policy of political parties may be established in a variety of ways, with the emphasis on policy coming from the bottom up, from the top down, or a combination of both. Whether the policy of the party is primarily decided by the leadership and handed out to the rank and file or whether it is decided by the party membership and handed in to the leaders, in both cases public opinion will have a considerable influence on its final form.

Obviously, unless it is a matter of fundamental principle, the party is unlikely to espouse causes which are unpopular with any significant degree of frequency if they wish to receive many votes. In my own experience, I have found that some of the best policies adopted by parties have sprung from ideas generated at the community level by persons in search of solutions to their own problems. How such ideas are translated into official policy varies with the practises and structures of the parties concerned. Other policies will be generated by "thinkers" in the various parties who will submit their ideas for adoption.

All parties adopt resolutions at their conventions or annual meetings, but some adopt so few—and those of such a "motherhood" nature—that it is impossible to avoid the feeling that they are less concerned with any real policy discussion by the membership than they are with staging a giant "pep" rally to impress the media. It is not difficult to spot such parties because these are the ones who will "unveil" their platforms a week or two after the election campaign has been in progress.

This releasing of party policy on the eve of an election has always bothered me since it seemed to indicate that there had been little or no on-going consideration of solid solutions to the problems of the day and, further, that the platform constituted something which had been "cooked up" at the last minute with the specific intention of attracting votes. These eleventh-hour platforms are invariably released from an executive or campaign committee meeting, further intimating that a very small number of persons had been responsible for its drafting and that the party membership had been little consulted.

In my own party the bulk of party policy is generated at the constituency level and becomes official through the mechanism of constituency resolutions being submitted to convention. The convention, comprised of delegates from all constituencies and affiliated organizations, will prioritize and then debate the resolutions. Those which receive the approval of a majority of the delegates will be incorporated into the party program which is then printed for public consumption. Consequently, when the election is announced our platform has been available for months previous; no "unveiling" is therefore necessary.

That is not to say, of course, that if new developments require changes in policy the party is straightjacketed and can do nothing about it: a Provincial Council of some 50 members may make policy when necessary between conventions and, on a day to day basis, the leader is, in effect, making new policy as he reacts to unfolding events.

Policy alone will not win elections. Money is needed and, if we can be guided by statistics, the more money the greater chance of success. To my mind this is a tragic fact of political life over which we should all be gravely concerned because the implication is that a party or an individual can buy their way into office.

While a great deal of party money is spent at the local level in paying poll workers and car drivers (except in the New Democratic Party, where this is forbidden by its constitution), the great bulk goes towards the purchase of advertising. In the 1974 Nova Scotia election, for example, the Liberal Party reported an expenditure of $172,000 on advertising, a figure representing some 86% of its total campaign budget. This would have gone to announcing meetings, large spreads in the newspapers and on radio and television commercials.

The power of advertising at election time should never be underestimated for the party which can afford to repeatedly push its message through the media has a greater chance of persuading people to support it at the polls. Conversely, the party (like my own, unfortunately) which cannot purchase as much time on radio or T.V. will suffer from having created the impression that it has dropped out of sight or is not serious. Consequently, money is most instrumental in deciding the outcome of the election.

It is perhaps interesting to note in this context that the degree of success enjoyed by each of the three parties in the 1974 election bore a significant relation to the amount of money they spent. Thus the Liberals, who reported a central provincial expenditure of $199,000, won; the Tories, who spent $183,000, formed the official opposition; and the New Democratic Party, as everyone knows, came third, having spent a mere $25,000.

There are two questions which must be answered in this respect. The first is: *should there be such a high level of election spending?* When one considers that at the local level there may have been as much as $20,000 spent, the total bill was well over a million dollars. At present there are restrictions on the amount of money which may be spent in elections, but they still allow for extremely generous expenditures and the reader must decide for himself whether or not they are too generous.

A more important question, however, is: *where does the money come from?* This question is posed by those who maintain that he who pays the piper calls the tune and that those who finance a political party will have a great deal of influence over its actions when it is elected to office.

New Democrats will say that since the vast bulk of the Tory and Grit election money comes from business—some of it from very big business—the actions of those parties will nearly always favour that sector of society. Liberals and Conservatives may reply that since the NDP gets some money from unions it will be dominated by "big labour". The fact of the matter is that the NDP gets relatively little from unions, relying heavily on the numerous but small donations of rank and file members; but in any event, the question of the influence over the party of the contributors is a serious and challenging one.

At present, candidates receiving more than 15% of the vote are entitled to a rebate from public funds, but there are those who argue that until election costs are completely financed from the public purse we will never have a true and fair democracy, because those with the money will call the tunes.

This leads directly to the question of patronage, about which there is always considerable public debate in Maritime politics. Crudely put, patronage is rewarding your friends and punishing your enemies. In its rankest form it would mean that government contracts for paving roads or building bridges would only go to companies which had contributed heavily to the campaign funds or whose principals were prominent members of the party in power, and that every government appointment would be filled by an active party supporter.

That some of this takes place is undeniable though hard to prove, but, thankfully it is nothing like it was even twenty or thirty years ago. The story of the Stanfield "massacre" of the Department of Highways when the Conservatives came to power in 1956 (when, reputedly, hundreds of employees were fired in one night and replaced by loyal Tories) is now firmly established in popular mythology if not in history, but it still goes on to an extent which is unacceptable.

However, it is important to note that not everything which looks like patronage *is* patronage. It is, for example, irresponsible to suggest that because a party supporter's company gets a contract it necessarily has been awarded simply for that reason. It is also unfair to automatically assume that a party supporter appointed to a government job possess no qualifications apart from his party membership. That does not mean it never happens, but it is dangerous to suggest it unless there is demonstrable evidence that politics has been the only deciding factor.

There are instances in which patronage of a kind will be inevitable and, in some cases, desirable. Where two applicants for a job have equal experience and qualifications, it is only realistic to suppose that the one whose political loyalty is to the government will get the nod; and, clearly, if one applicant among a number of equally qualified individuals is known as a virulent opponent of the government, it is reasonable to suppose that he will not be appointed. Also, there will be a number of key, policy, and decision-making positions in government where the administration will want to appoint persons who share its political philosophy and its goals.

A government which appointed to these important and confidential jobs known opponents would likely find many of its plans and policies being sabotaged from within, not to mention sensitive material being leaked to the opposition.

Let me stress at this point that in the preceding I have not been speaking of the civil service, which has, and should have, strict rules and procedures of hiring, but of usually senior appointments to boards, agencies and commissions. In some of these cases, my criticisms have not been so much that the appointees were government supporters but that the administration had picked such poor and untalented supporters!

What is clearly reprehensible, in my view, is the firing or hiring of highway employees, casual workers, game wardens, licence vendors and the like simply on the basis of party affiliation. This is senseless and inhumane and, ultimately, I believe, politically counterproductive. It is to be hoped that this practise, already on the decline, will, together with election bribery, soon be a thing of the past.

Jeremy Akerman

"LOFTY TONES"
DAVID LEWIS – A POWERFUL ORATOR

10: Pros and Cons

This final chapter is designed to outline as fairly as possible the benefits and disadvantages of being an elected member in order to enable those who may be thinking about taking the plunge to make up their minds, and to assist the politician hunters in deciding whether they should fill us full of buckshot or give us another chance.

The life of a politician is stimulating and varied, full of new faces, new events and unpredictable ones at that. This, in itself, is worth a great deal to be freed, at least to some extent, from the boring routine of many people's daily work. No matter what drawbacks there may be to being in politics, compared with the daily rut of an assembly line worker, for instance, the life of a politician is heaven if you are the type who can take the pace and the pressure.

Being involved in committees and conferences can bring to the elected member a knowledge and understanding of many aspects of life denied to the average person. Meeting highly-interesting and sometimes famous people does not fall to the average citizen, yet elected members may frequently have such an opportunity.

Jeremy Akerman

Few people get the chance to travel abroad and some get little chance to travel outside the province, but elected members often have these chances. Members of all parties in Nova Scotia have travelled to conferences in Ontario, Quebec and the western provinces and some have even been lucky enough to travel to some exotic foreign countries.

The Speaker, for example, has visited a number of countries, including Australia, to study the ways in which their parliaments are operated. The Leader of the Opposition led a small delegation to the Caribbean nations in 1975, while the Premier has visited a host of countries, including Yugoslavia, Ceylon, Samoa, India, France and Germany.

In my six years in the Legislature I have had one such trip, when the Premier, the Leader of the Opposition and myself represented the province at a function in London. Government members get more of these junkets than opposition members, but, sooner or later, most members will be offered a trip which they probably would not take were they not elected members.

There are also the financial benefits involved in being elected to office. The ordinary MLA in Nova Scotia currently receives $14,400 a year, of which $4,800 is tax free. He is also allowed eighteen trips between Halifax and his constituency per year and one per week while the House is in session, at 19.2 cents per mile. In addition he is allowed a maximum of up to $35 per day while the House is sitting to cover hotel, meals and transportation if he lives more than 25 miles from the House.

The Premier gets $39,400, the cabinet ministers and the Leader of the Opposition $35,400, the Speaker $25,400, the leader of a recognized third party $20,400 and the Deputy Speaker $17,900.

If a member also has another source of income, say from a business, law or medical practise, the members' pay represents a seemingly welcome lump of pocket money, although it must be remembered that with legal fees and doctors' incomes the way they are today, members who are doctors and lawyers may, in some cases, actually be losing money if the session of the House is a particularly long one.

From the above it will be clearly seen that no member of the House is going to starve, and for federal Members of Parliament that eventuality is even more remote. The pay and benefits of M.P.s in Ottawa can, in my opinion, only be described as generous. At Ottawa the M.P.s get $34,600, of which $10,600 is tax free. The Prime Minister gets $67,600, his cabinet ministers receiving $54,600. In addition, there are very comfortable pension benefits and a host of other expense items, perquisites and concessions.

I have taken the trouble to outline this in some detail because large numbers of the public think that provincial MLAs get paid the same as their counterparts in Ottawa. There is, as we have seen, no comparison and it is important to note that some provincial members feel the MLAs do more work and are exposed to greater pressures and a greater volume of individual complaints simply because they are accessible and closer to the people (a contention, I might add, that will be hotly contested by the M.P.s!).

In addition to the straight monetary benefits of being an elected member there are a large number of free meals, but they can only be considered an advantage if you like eating out and have an abnormal partiality for dry turkey, potato salad and canned peas.

There is also that indefinable advantage conferred upon the elected member which enables him to command a little more respect than he otherwise would and claim a little more status than he previously possessed. There are some to whom this is terribly important, but in my view it is rather meaningless and over-rated. (When I was first elected I received an invitation to join a private club, whose secretary informed me that since I was good enough to have been elected I was now able to meet their standards. I told them what they could do with their invitation!)

Readers are not entitled to assume that the flow of money is all one way, for a great deal of that which the member receives is paid out again on a variety of things unconnected with his personal comfort. He will be expected to contribute to his political party, to the United Appeal, the Salvation Army, the Heart Fund, the Little League, the broom ball, junior hockey, the Kidney Foundation, and the Mile of Money; and unless his donation is large the word

What Have You Done for Me Lately?

will get around that he is cheap. In recent years I have made a practise of contributing meaningful sums to a few charities which have special significance to me, but am still approached on a regular basis for every fund-raising project imaginable.

In addition, the member will be required to shell out to help families who have been burned out, buy the occasional grocery order for those who have been unable to get welfare, pay rent for persons on the verge of eviction and dip into his pocket for the "stemmers" at every street corner. In addition, his position requires above average expenditures on clothes, travel, telephone and postage so, while his income is decent, his expenses are high.

The real price paid by the elected member is in the loss of his privacy and in having to contend with some very strange persons and situations. Anyone to whom privacy is all important would be most unhappy in politics, as telephone calls at two in the morning and interruptions during meals may be regular occurrences. In addition, the member may be unable to quietly enjoy himself at a theatre or club because he will be recognized and be regaled with a problem—or worse, be picked on by an inebriated person who wants to show off in front of his friends.

A member taking the sun on the beach on Dominion Day might be gently prodded by someone who thinks it is an ideal opportunity to discuss his mother's pension case. A member who gently informs a caller that he is in the middle of his supper (this actually happened to me one day) may be told "tell the wife to put it back in the oven."

Similarly, if bizarre situations and requests would be undesirable to a person, politics is not for him. I have already mentioned the call at 2:30 am in connection with a train which had left the rails. Clearly the caller expected me to pull on my boots and get down there with a crow bar!

At about three o'clock in the morning on Christmas Day I received a long distance collect call from a man who roundly abused me because he had learned that the local Air Canada business office would be closed that day. On another occasion a man insisted I get him the Widows Allowance. I explained that he was ineligible because he was not a widow, but obviously dissatisfied, he went away muttering that the woman next door had got it so why couldn't he? A woman caller one day demanded I obtain a Kentucky Fried Chicken franchise for her, but, fortunately was most understanding when I explained that it was hardly within my power or jurisdiction to do so. Another man asked me to get him a divorce. When I outlined the only possible form of assistance I could think of he did not think the idea a very good one!

Most frustrating and disappointing of all to an elected member, I think, is the occurrence of those one has helped turning against one. Some of the people on whose problems the member has spent the most time and effort may be the very people who are working hardest against him in the next election. This is democracy, but it still hurts. I have found that

What Have You Done for Me Lately?

some (fortunately very few) people for whom I have gone out of my way to an extraordinary extent and at personal expense have been those who have been most vocal in condemning me around town.

Speaking of personal expense, my colleagues and I have numerous experiences of having shelled out considerable sums from our own pockets to help people in trouble, never to hear from them again. Persons who have been evicted from their dwellings often cannot obtain new accommodation unless they have a month's rent in advance and if they are poor or unemployed they cannot raise the rent. Often I have extended the month's rent, asking them to repay me if and when they are able, explaining that if they cannot do so it will be all right if they call and tell me so. Seldom have I ever heard from them thereafter.

The real reward of being in public life lies in the satisfaction in knowing that one is not sitting helpless on the sidelines watching events unfold, but is in there trying, for better or worse, to influence those events and that one has a say in the people's assembly which has been so precious to our way of life for centuries. Even greater reward than that is to be found in learning that one's efforts on behalf of a person have been successful, especially when that person acknowledges the help.

Sometimes, after a harrowing and frustrating day, when it is late at night and I am wondering what I am doing in this crazy business, a single telephone call can completely transform my mood from one of gloom to one of joy. A woman calls: "I wanted you to know that my daughter's student loan has been increased. We know that if you hadn't taken the case to Halifax she would not have been able to go to college. We'll never forget you."

I go to bed knowing that politics can be a noble profession and that it is all worthwhile.

About the author

Jeremy Akerman is an adoptive Nova Scotian who has lived in the province for 58 years (as of 2022). In that time he has been an archaeologist, a radio announcer, a politician, a senior civil servant, a newspaper editor and a film actor.

He is painter of landscapes and portraits, a singer of Irish folk songs, a lover of wine, and a devotee of history, especially of the British Labour Party.